GIVING VOICE to LINNENTOWN

★ ★ ★

GIVING VOICE *to* LINNENTOWN

★ ★ ★

HATTIE THOMAS WHITEHEAD

Cover design by Ivica Jandrijevic
Interior layout and design by www.writingnights.org
Book preparation by Chad Robertson
Edited by:
Elayne Wells Harmer (Executive Editor)
Elizabeth Bernstein
Joseph Carter
Marie Eddins
Cynthia F. Jackson
Barbara Oliver
Andrea Renee Price

ISBN: 978-0-578-91290-5
LIBRARY OF CONGRESS CATALOGING-IN-PUBLICATION DATA:
NAMES: Whitehead, Hattie Thomas., author
TITLE: Giving Voice to Linnentown / Hattie Thomas Whitehead
IDENTIFIERS: ISBN 9780578912905 (Perfect bound) |
ISBN 9780578912929 (eBook)
SUBJECTS: | Non-Fiction | History | Social Justice | Memoir
CLASSIFICATION: Pending
LC record pending

Published by Tiny Tots & Tikes, 2021
Printed in the United States of America on acid-free paper.

24   23   22   21   8   7   6   5   4   3   2   1

Dedication

For my mother and father,
Abe Thomas and Laura Maude Thomas Day,
and for my siblings,
Abe Thomas Jr., Katie Thomas Wilson, Andrew Thomas,
Linda Thomas, Marion Craft, and Alexander Thomas

EPIGRAPH

"Do not be silent; there is no limit to the power that may be released through you."

Howard Thurman
Deep is the Hunger: Meditations for Apostles of Sensitiveness

Contents

Foreword

Athens has a rich history, but it is the history of the rich. The concept of the University of Georgia was formed by a group of legislators in 1785 and would eventually become the nation's first land-grant institution. Clarke County was established in 1801 and named after Elijah Clarke, a Revolutionary War hero, and Athens was established as a town in 1805. But by 1860, half of the population in Clarke County were slaves. Still today, in 2021, you can speak to residents whose families worked on plantations in the surrounding areas and hear the stories they tell about the hardships their parents and grandparents faced.

After the Civil War, a black middle class emerged and flourished for close to half a century with local legends like Pink Morton of the Morton Theatre and Dr. William H. Harris, a prominent black physician. This prosperity during Reconstruction was to be short-lived, and the rising popularity of policies like segregation, Jim Crow, and "separate but equal" eroded the self-esteem and confidence of an already oppressed population even further. During this time, Georgia led the nation in racial genocide at the hands of lynch mobs. It is against this backdrop that in 1961, the University of Georgia was integrated by Charlayne Hunter and Hamilton Holmes.

As a young boy, I remember the son of civil rights icon James Meredith telling me stories of the integration of the University of Mississippi. There were riots and protests in Mississippi and Georgia when black students enrolled for the first time at both universities. One day, Mr. Meredith walked down a tree-lined street and was shot in the back with air rifles. Even though I was just thirteen, when I met Mr. Meredith I knew I was meeting history itself. Ms. Hunter and Mr. Holmes also endured rage and hatred from the white student body. Meanwhile, the State of Georgia had another plan for its black population in Athens, one that would destroy the very fiber of Black families and erase generational wealth and opportunity they had cobbled together with blood, sweat, and tears.

It has been well established that in this country, the quickest and best way to create wealth is through homeownership. In my earliest memory of my grandmother Fannie Mae Gandy Price, she said, "Don't sell your land, because it's the only thing they don't make more of." Land is what drove the United States into existence and still drives wealth-building to this very day. But opportunities for land ownership have been systematically taken away from America's Black population. Policies like exclusionary zoning laws, redlining enforced by the Federal Housing Authority, and a G.I. Bill that favored White home ownership over Black home ownership exacerbated the already existing racial wealth gap which we still see today. But the coup de grâce was the policy of urban renewal: the actual condemnation of and taking of people's property under the guise of "removal of slum and blight."

One hundred years after Vice President of the Confederate States of America Alexander Hamilton Stephens gave his famous Cornerstone Speech in Savannah, Georgia, in 1861—in which he defended slavery and reiterated that the foundation of the Confederacy was the inferiority of Blacks to Whites—our public institutions of higher education were integrated. Only one year later, as if in response to that integration, the federal government, working in conjunction with Georgia elected officials, forced the sale of homes owned by Black citizens of Athens. They were paid less than their White counterparts for more valuable property, and were unable to purchase new homes in certain areas. Families were broken apart as generational roots were ripped out of the ground, and some were forced to move into public housing and to rely on the very government that had betrayed them.

Giving Voice to Linnentown is just a slice of that vast and dark history. It is the history of one family who could see the hashmarks on the football field from their neighborhood. It is the history of one twelve-year-old girl whose family home was burned to the ground as an intimidation tactic for other homeowners who had held out against the pressure of the forced sale. How these families endured these trials and tribulations is the epitome of the American spirit: true American grit. How else can one describe the success of achieving the American Dream not once, but twice? And when that twelve-year-old girl grew up to have a family and a home of her own, her own daughter attended that once-segregated university and married a football player who played in the stadium on the very field they saw from their backyards.

Our history belongs to all of us, not just the rich, and these stories must be told and remembered, for it is our burden to teach future generations of our mistakes, lest they be repeated.

Representative Spencer R. Frye
House District 118
Athens, Georgia

Acknowledgements

I came to the conclusion that I needed to write this book after a number of presentations, interviews, and forums about Linnentown. It seemed there was never enough time to give a good overview of how we lived there. I wanted to give details of families' interactions, where we played as children, and the games we played. I wanted to explain the expectation of all children in the community to be respectful to all adults: no talking back. I wanted to describe the working skills of our women and men and how they used these skills to repair whatever was broken when a neighbor reached out to them. I wanted to tell stories of the leadership and support adults gave to neighborhood children who needed wheels or planks to build a small contraption or big pigeon cage. I wanted to praise the successfulness of the neighborhood in reaching 66 percent property ownership on meager wages.

I wanted to tell the stories of Linnentown.

I dedicate this book to my parents, Abe Thomas and Laura Maude Crawford Thomas Day. It is also a tribute to all my relatives and other residents who lived in Linnentown, who spent years in turmoil after an "urban renewal" sign was erected on South Finley Street. This book chronicles families and children before and during urban renewal, and the effect on my family after we moved from the community.

Special thanks to my daughter, Rev. Cynthia Faye Jackson, for encouraging me to write this book. I'm grateful for the support of my nieces Barbara Oliver, Rhonda Marie Eddins, and Andrea Renee Price. Thank you to Dr. Joseph Carter for personal support and for research data that I used in this book. Thank you, Rachelle Berry, for your support and for assisting with the research. Thank you to my long-time friend Elizabeth Bernstein for editing this book and for the support she gave me during this time. Thank you to my Executive Editor, Elayne Wells Harmer, for overseeing this project and for all your hard work.

And finally, a special thank you to Athens-Clarke County Commissioner Mariah Parker for championing our resolution and my community.

Prologue

My name is Hattie Thomas Whitehead. I was born on July 17, 1948, in a small Black neighborhood the residents called "Linnentown," although the city of Athens, Georgia, has no official name on record. It was nestled among White communities on all four sides. Linnentown was located about four blocks from the University of Georgia (UGA) stadium and was made up of three streets: South Finley, Lyndon Row, and Peabody Street.

Linnentown residents were skilled laborers: brick masons, carpenters, beauticians, a nurse, cooks, construction workers, janitors, and housekeepers. We even had a professional baseball player! By 1960, this community had about fifty families with 66 percent property ownership, which they accomplished by carefully saving while working for meager wages for many years. We were building our wealth slowly but surely despite nearly insurmount-able obstacles that Black property owners had in our commu-nity—and everywhere in the South.

But then, in 1962, the University of Georgia and city of Ath-ens received a federal grant through the Federal Urban Renewal Program to demolish our neighborhood. We were called a "slum," so they simply kicked us out and erased Linnentown. This happy place was where I lived for fourteen years with my parents, Abe Thomas and Laura Maude Crawford Thomas, and my six siblings: Abe Jr., Katie, Andrew ("Pepper"), Linda ("Pete"), Marion, and Alex. Today, it is a UGA parking lot.

This is my story of how it happened.

Chapter One
FAMILY LIFE IN LINNENTOWN

In Linnentown, there were no sidewalks or streetlights in our community. Only one streetlight was at the end of our neighborhood on Cloverhurst, where we played until dusk or until the streetlight came on. South Finley, Lyndon Row, and our portion of Peabody Street were partially paved; however, the portion of Peabody in the White neighborhood was completely paved. That's the only portion still existing today. The tar abruptly stopped before connecting to our part of Finley, as if the city had suddenly decided to not send the work crew back to finish the job.

Because there were no well-lit areas, we used front yards for playing games. Alex, the baby of our family, and his friends Bobby Crook and Bobby Thrasher shot marbles, threw rocks at cans or bottles, climbed trees, and spent long hours shooting basketballs through a rim nailed to a tree. Hopscotch required us to get a stick and mark off blocks with numbers. After the number of squares were marked off, a shooter, bottle cap, or rock was placed on the first square. Then the player would hop on one leg into single blocks, jump with spread legs into side-by-side blocks, right leg in one, left in the other, continue to hop through the hopscotch until the end, turn around, hop back to the shooter, and pick it up. Then it was the next person's turn. After each turn, the shooter would be placed in the next higher-number block. If a player's foot touched a line, that player would be out. The game continued until there was a winner.

My eldest brother, Abe, spent a lot of time with his friends playing in the water at the creek. One summer day in 1956, Abe decided to set up a play area. All his friends agreed and pitched in to help, and they worked on a plan for several days. As soon as they completed the play area, Abe ran home and shouted to me and a few others, "Y'all come to the creek to see what we've done! It's a big surprise!"

We followed closely, hurriedly, whispering to each other, "What in the world have they done?!"

Tall bushes lined both sides of the final stretch to the creek area, making walking difficult. Briar patches scratched our legs as we made our way. After the final few steps, we entered a wide open space that Abe and his friends had cleared, giving us a view of the creek's opposite bank.

Wow! I thought. I hadn't seen it before because of all the bushes.

I looked up at a long bundle of vines hanging over a tree limb about twenty-four feet from the ground and wondered if this was Abe's big surprise. I kept staring, still clueless about the excitement bubbling up in him. Abe looked at me expectantly with a big smile on his face, but I didn't get it.

"It's a swing to get to the other side of the creek and back!" he explained.

After Abe showed what the bundle of vines was and how we would use it, a smile started spreading on my face, then I erupted in giggles. I pointed at the swing, open-mouthed, my eyes wide. He grabbed my hand and said, "Let me take you across, Hattie!"

With no hesitation, I circled my arms around his waist and held on tightly. I figured we would either both get to the other side or both fall in the creek. I was not going to let go of him. Holding the swing in both hands, Abe stepped back to get momentum, then jumped off. I hung onto him like a baby opossum latched on to her mother's back, laughing and whooping while we swung in midair over the creek. He landed on the other side with both feet, and only then did I loosen my grip. What a ride!

We all took turns swinging back and forth, laughing the whole time, and we played until dusk. I loved playing at the creek, although I couldn't swing to the other side alone. There was no knot for my hands to grip, and my hands were not wide enough to grip the vines. But just being there at the water's edge was enough. The older teenagers had spent long hours fashioning an area at the creek where children could just play. This little area allowed us the freedom to explore, imaginatively turning our ordinary landscape into a wonderland of bliss.

I admired Abe so much. He was confidant, smart, adventurous, and delightfully spontaneous. One day he abruptly decided that he loved pigeons, so he and some friends built an outdoor bird cage with wire and leftover wood that some neighbors gave him. This birdcage was about 12' x 10' in size and included a flimsy door that had to be propped closed with a brick, and the sides and top were covered with wire. Abe cleared out an area in the back for the pigeons to lay eggs, and told us of his elaborate plans as we listened attentively.

According to Abe, there was a church on Milledge Ave with a loft that had been vacant for quite some time. He and a couple of friends would be catching these birds at night in the church loft. Once we returned home, Abe walked straight to our closet, took out some pillowcases, and explained how he would place the pigeons inside them.

After bedtime one night, he decided it was "pigeon-catching time." He snuck out, then returned home while we were all asleep. The next morning, he woke us up with great excitement.

"Follow me to the pigeon cage!" he said. We got dressed and followed, but I was so puzzled. How did he catch them at night? When we reached the cage, we saw about six pigeons flying around. We erupted with delight. We had never been this close to birds before!

Abe started pointing out distinct but small differences in the coloring of each one. While talking, he opened the door of the cage and encouraged us to step inside. We entered reluctantly. The pigeons were flying around as we stood just inside the door, still amazed that we were standing so close to them, all the while ducking down as the pigeons flew overhead. We were enjoying this immensely.

From then on, Abe allowed us to enter the cage with him to feed them, and, sometimes, to hold the small ones. After a few months passed, the number of birds had increased with each nightly trip to the church and with the birth of new birds. Dad had to intervene.

"Stop the night trips, son," he said to Abe. "You have enough birds to take care of and enjoy."

"Yes, sir," Abe replied. He enjoyed looking at them and

pointing out the differences to us. We loved it as well.

My baby sister, Marion, and her playmates Rena and Shirley often played hide-and-seek or jackstones. If they did not have the jacks and only a ball, the replacements were small rocks. I loved playing hand-clap games that included singing "Miss Mary Mack" while popping my fingers. Adding the finger-popping and creating rhymes for the song made the hand game more interesting. I also enjoyed jumping rope. Creating different routines made it fun, especially if two jumped at the same time. My best friend and playmate was Evelyn Taylor. She was always fun to play with and never disagreeable. I enjoyed playing at the creek, but the community baseball games were the best.

The ball games were played in an open field behind Jeruel Academy/Union Institute. This was a Black private school that closed in the late 1950s. Freddie Mae Brown Jackson, Christine Davis Johnson, and my siblings Abe and Katie attended school there for a short time. We met at the field at a designated time in late afternoon and selected two persons to be captains. They would choose players for their teams and then flip a coin to determine which team would go first.

We played baseball for hours. We played game after game until dusk, when we couldn't see the ball anymore. It wasn't important who won or lost—we just had fun playing the game. Some days, after a baseball game, the girls would enter the office of the Academy and play "school." Even though the school had been closed for a long time, there were still file cabinets with papers inside. We pulled the papers out and played "school" with them.

In the evenings, we played hide-and-seek, but the rules we had then were a bit different from today's. Once the seeker was chosen and we had identified a "safe" pole or bush, we would race to go hide, then race back out of hiding and touch the chosen place, which allowed a "safe" call. The seeker would count to twenty and then start to seek. Depending on how many were playing and how dark it was, the game could last for thirty minutes or more. If our parents started calling our names, we stopped the games, and home we went. We had to be back before dark.

There were some more daring adventures in the neighborhood. My brother Pepper was the most competitive sibling among us and truly enjoyed racing his wagon. Riding his wagon full speed from the hilltop of Peabody Street to the bottom fueled his competitiveness. He spent many daytime hours riding his wagon down Peabody, jumping off after stopping, and jogging back up the hill while pulling the wagon behind him. In hopes of increased speed, Pepper honed his technique of a quick leg push-off while steering the wagon handle with one hand, controlling the two front wheels. Any sudden movement of the wheels or any weight shift would flip the wagon over and throw Pepper out. But even after he'd go flying out of the wagon, he demonstrated amazing resilience, getting up with scratches on his arms and legs from sliding on the tarred street. Mom had to put two to three patches on his pants due to his rough play. When Pepper made it to the end of the street, the wagon slowed down where the tar on Peabody ended. The wheels would made contact with the dirt, and the wagon and rider rolled directly into the bushes, bringing the ride to a sudden stop.

Pepper repeated this wagon ride over and over again, always asking for a challenger. When another wagon rider showed up, Pepper challenged, "I've got the faster wagon! Wanna race?" Most declined due to having many previous losses. After weeks of hilltop racing with wagon turnovers, wheels rolling in the dirt, and bushes bringing the rider to an abrupt stop, the wagon was damaged beyond repair.

After a few weeks without a usable wagon, Pepper decided to salvage parts from it and build a wooden race cart. He confiscated wood and other items from Dad and neighbors and built a new race cart in a couple of weeks. Pepper was so proud of what he had accomplished. This race cart had wheels that allowed it to go faster than his old one. This new wooden "race wagon" was definitely in a league of its own. The only downside was that he had no one to race! However, he still enjoyed riding it because it was fast. He continued to get scrapes and bruises but had no serious injuries.

Catching and releasing snakes was another pastime Pepper shared with friends. He'd catch snakes in half-gallon glass jars with holes in a metal top and walk inside the house with a jar behind his back. We girls would be sitting together in the living room talking. Pepper would walk in with a smile on his face, not saying a word, and pull out his arm. When we saw the snake inside the jar, we'd immediately start screaming and running. We'd knocked over chairs as we ran into the kitchen where Mom was cooking. We would stand behind her, still screaming, "He got a snake! He got a snake!" all the while pointing to the living room.

"Pepper, get out of this house with that snake!" Mom would yell sternly.

She'd have a dish cloth in her hand and would start swinging it at him as he was backing out the front door. Mom would forbid him to come inside until Dad came home later that night. Dad would have a long, long talk with Pepper outside, and when they came in, Dad would assure us that Pepper wouldn't bring another snake home again. However, that wasn't a promise Pepper would keep.

My sister Pete played at the creek most summer days along with the rest of us, and she was the only one to have a serious accident there. One day, we were playing in the creek water or on the swing, when suddenly there was loud screaming, followed by crying, which brought everything to a sudden stop. Looking around, I saw that Pete was crying while looking at her foot. Pepper quickly raced to her and saw blood oozing from Pete's foot. Pepper picked her up and started running toward home, the rest of us running behind him. One of the boys looked in the grass and found a large piece of glass with smears of blood.

"She cut her foot on a piece of glass!" he yelled.

After reaching home, Pepper began explaining what happened while Dad examined Pete's foot. Due to the depth and length of the cut, Dad thought stitches were needed. He put Pete in the car, and off to the emergency room they went. We all had to wait patiently for their return. She returned with a smile on her face, showing us her foot that had been bandaged so well, we couldn't see her foot at all!

"You can't go back to the creek until your foot heals," Dad warned her. A few of us stayed and played on the porch that day and the following days until her foot healed.

The creek was preferable to our designated pre-integration swimming pool built by the City of Athens in the trash dump of New Town, another Athens Black community. It was embarrassing swimming there. We could see the tractors pushing the trash all over the area while we swam. We all wanted a pool, but why build one in the city's trash dump? This was how the city disregarded the Black children in Athens. It was not right, but we had no one to advocate for us.

A more pleasant summer pastime was picking wild blackberries. A few of us kids decided on a time and meeting place. From there, we'd walk about three miles across the University of Georgia campus to a road near the railroad tracks. Not far off the road was a long blackberry patch with big, juicy blackberries. We wore long sleeves to protect our arms from the thorns and carried our buckets to the blackberry patch. We ate as many as we picked. Our motivation was blackberry cobblers. My mother made the best— it never lasted more than ten minutes after she removed it from the oven. We licked every ounce of juice from the cobbler's pan.

While summertime gave us freedom to explore outside, we also stretched our imaginations in school. Marion's favorite subject in school was English. Her handwriting was so pretty on paper that a couple of teachers asked her to write documents that were going to be displayed at school. Marion also had musical talent— she loved singing rhythm & blues and dancing. At home, she sang all the time, sometimes orchestrating and creating dance moves in step with the music.

One day at Lyons Middle School, the principal asked all teachers to recommend a child to represent their school and compete at a district talent show. One of Marion's teachers had observed her dancing during recess and complimented her, so she asked her to be involved in their school competition, which could lead to the county competition if she won. Marion agreed to participate and immediately started working on her dance routines. She performed her dance routine perfectly at the competition and won first place. She also won the county's competition and brought home a trophy for her school. This was such a proud moment for her, her school, and her family. What an honor! After each event, Marion repeated details to all of us as we sat at the dinner table, listening and asking questions while we ate. We were all very proud of her accomplishments.

Pete took pride in being a member of the school band and performing on a flute she received one year as a gift. After examining it, she attempted to figure out how to play. About two months later, the unpleasant noise started sounding good to our ears. It appeared that she was musically inclined, and she played her flute effortlessly. After school started, she joined the band and was introduced to flute music sheets. I often watched her practice, mesmerized by how she moved her fingers while blowing across the flute's holes with her mouth. The songs she played on her flute had nice sounds but were unfamiliar to me; however, she liked them.

My older sister Katie loved rock and roll music. One Christmas, she received a small black record player with a radio, and it played continuously for the next week. Katie put a chair next to our bed and placed the record player there. Waking after midnight each night, Katie slowly turned the radio dial, listening as she searched for a rhythm & blues station out of Nashville, Tennessee. We found it most nights, and I listened while slowly falling off to sleep—only to be awakened by Katie when the station played a song that was popular.

She loved to dance and looked forward to going to the YWCA every Friday night for the weekly dance. The Y was located in Rocksprings Homes, and it was the place to be on Friday nights. It cost twenty-five cents to enter and listen to popular music played by the DJ, Raymond Rountree. Chairs lined the walls on all sides of the building, and the girls sat until a boy walked over and held his hand out to a girl, which meant, "Please dance with me." Girls almost always danced with a boy when asked.

Katie and I also loved going to the movies together. Initially, the balcony at the Georgia Theater in downtown Athens was set aside for Blacks. In later years, we attended the Sol Abrams's Harlem Theater on Broad Street once it was opened for us. Mrs. Julia Linston was always there, willing and eager to sell tickets. This was the place to be on Saturdays or Sundays.

Dad fostered our interests. Alex once found a ball in some bushes near the community and he brought it home.

"What kind of ball is this?" he asked Dad. "What's it used for?"

"It's a billiard ball," Dad answer. "You need fifteen of them to play a game of pool."

Dad continued describing the table, pool sticks, and rules of the game. Alex listened intently. When Dad finished with all the details, he promised to take Alex to a pool room so he could observe the game and understand in depth how it's played. One day, Dad came home with a long, round, slender wooden handle. We asked him what he was going to do with it, and he replied, "It's a pool stick, and it's for Alex."

Later, when Alex came inside, Dad handed it to him and explained what it was and how to use it. A big smile lit up Alex's face. Dad reached for the pool stick while Alex was standing close by and placed the ball on our kitchen table to demonstrate the correct positioning of the hand and fingers on the stick. With a quick thrust of his arm, the pool stick made contact with the ball, which moved with such high speed we all jumped back in amazement. My brother was astonished. Dad smiled and promised Alex a trip to the pool room soon. Meanwhile, Alex managed to practice handling the stick on an old wooden table with raised edges on all four sides. He spent a great deal of time with this stick and one billiard ball.

One morning, Dad announced that they were going to the pool room. When they got back, he told us all about it. First, they had sat and observed a couple of games. As Alex asked questions, Dad explained each answer in great detail. He was amazed at how attentive Alex was. When it was their turn to play, Dad talked Alex through the game. He was so impressed with Alex's ability to handle the pool stick. Dad said that Alex's playing with that one ball on the old table had enabled him to shoot the pool stick with some accuracy at breaking the balls. Alex was all smiles, proudly listening to Dad tell us of their experience at the pool room.

Late one evening, a couple of months later, we were all home when Dad came inside with a small table. He placed it on the dining table and announced that it was a pool table for Alex. When Alex heard these words, he jumped up from the floor and sprinted over. Dad looked down at him and said, "Now you can learn how to play pool." Alex was speechless as he looked at the table in shock. Dad placed his hand on Alex's shoulder and said, "Now let's get all the pool items from the car."

Alex played on that pool table every day and allowed us to play with him as long as we followed his instructions. He gave us strict orders to not touch or play on this table if he wasn't there. Whenever I babysat him, we played pool.

Besides playing, we children had chores and were expected to help out in the community. When we lived on Finley, Katie and I walked everywhere. She always held my hand, not just part of the way but until we reached our destination. The entire time we were walking, my small hand was inside hers. I always loved walking and talking with her. She was my big sister, and I felt safe with her. We had to walk everywhere, as Dad's car was for his and Mom's own use, not to drive us places. We walked to the grocery store in downtown Athens to pay bills for our parents or other grown-ups in the neighborhood and to visit Katie's friends. Whenever we walked to downtown, we always stopped by the A&A Bakery on Lumpkin. With whatever dimes and nickels we had, we'd buy day-old donuts. That was always a treat. A white bag held our sweet treats, which we ate as we walked back home. We got plenty of exercise!

Walking to school each day, though, was challenging. Crossing Baxter Street and then Broad Street involved running at the first break in traffic, for there were no traffic lights at any point of crossing. The older children would help us younger ones, since cars were always speeding. Holding hands to cross these dangerous streets was essential to avoid being hit by a car.

On Saturdays, we faced this hazard to get to Edward's grocery store, where one or two of us would accompany our mother, pushing the shopping cart loaded with the week's groceries. She would often stop and talk with neighbors who were also at the store, which prolonged her grocery shopping time. Before any checking-out could be done for groceries, last week's grocery bill had to be paid in full, or some type of payment arrangement was agreed upon. Afterward, Mrs. Edwards started putting in the cost of each item into an adding machine. After everything was totaled up, the groceries were bagged. This was the payment and charge cycle each week.

During the week, if we needed an item from the grocery store, our mother wrote a note on a piece of paper, and one of us would carry it to the store and give it to Mrs. Edwards. She would get the item from a shelf, pull out a small general-purpose book, write numbers in it, bag the item, and hand it to us. The only communication that took place was a "hello."

If I had a nickel or a dime, I couldn't wait to buy a candy bar. I liked Baby Ruth candy bars, mainly due to their size. I would eat my Baby Ruth slowly because it tasted so good. Other times, I would only eat half and save the other half for later. I also liked the taste of Zero candy bars. On the counter, Mrs. Edwards always kept a big, see-through plastic container of butter cookies. They were twice the size of butter cookies today and could be purchased with pennies. They were big and delicious, and this was the alternative if I only had pennies in my hand.

It was a delight on Saturdays when the vegetable truck would come to our neighborhood. Everyone looked forward to buying fresh vegetables and chatting with Mr. Sidney Thurmond and his wife, Vanilla. He would slowly drive his truck down the street, blowing his horn. This alerted all to come out and look over the vegetables. Some of them were purchased in bunches and others were weighed. We would always exchange greetings before making any purchases. Sometimes, a few of the neighborhood women shared recipes or food.

In our house, the chores were not divided; only the daughters had them. Washing dishes was my sister Katie's and my responsibility. She would heat the water on top of the stove, for we had no hot running water. I would separate the dishes and stack them. Katie would start washing, and I would dry and put them away. This was considered a girl's responsibility, to which we often objected, to no avail. There were always mountains of dirty clothes to be washed and clean clothes to be folded and put away.

Another chore was assigned to the girls was hanging washed clothes on the clotheslines. We did not have a clothes dryer. Drying clothes involved carrying a wash tub of wet, clean clothes to the clotheslines. On top of the clothes was a medium-sized bag of wooden clothespins. Our clotheslines were constructed with a long 14-gauge wire line attached to two wooden posts. Each piece of clothing had to be hung and anchored with wooden pins which prevented the clothes from blowing to the ground or into our neighbors' yards. When they were dry (the amount of time depended on whether there was direct sunlight or wind), we took them off the clotheslines and carried them inside, then folded and put them away. This was no small chore, but somehow it was also always the girls' responsibility.

Besides washing dishes and doing laundry, I pitched in to keep the floors clean. Every household had a string mop and a straw broom. A broom was multipurpose, used for sweeping floors inside and out, killing bugs, removing spider webs, beating rugs on the clotheslines, and so on. When all the strings were gone from a mop or straw from a broom, these tools were not thrown out—the handles were cut down and then used to prop windows up, allowing fresh air inside the house.

The mop and its bucket were kept in the kitchen or back porch, always filled with soapy water ready for mopping floors on rainy days in summer months. We were careful not to forget the bucket of soapy water. If left too many days, it had an awful smell when the mop and bucket were needed again. Mopping was a real chore to me, particularly in the winter months. I dreaded hearing those four words from Mom: "Hattie, get the mop." Before retrieving it, I could visualize the strings frozen solid, which would lead to tedious steps of thawing: pouring a kettle of boiling hot water over the strings inside the bucket, then repeating the steps until the strings were wringable. This had to be done before any mopping could take place. I knew what I had to do while putting on my coat to get started.

We children knew about the importance of completing chores and hard work from watching the adults around us, especially my father and mother. My dad was not raised by his parents, but by another family on a farm in Greene County, Georgia. He often spoke about how he was raised, plowing a field at daybreak, then walking miles to his school. He managed to reach third grade before being pulled out to help more on the farm.

Because of his commitment to hard work, he did not believe in letting us sleep in. If he left for an early appointment on Saturday or Sunday mornings and came back home before 7:00 am, he'd shout out, "Why are you all still in bed?" We had to get up right then and wouldn't dare take our time, or his next words would be, "Make haste!" We were expected to be up and about, doing some type of activity around the house, so he could settle down. His famous words were, "When I was on the farm, I would've plowed a field by now."

At twenty-one, Dad moved to Athens, spending a lot of time with his cousin Fat on Callaway Corner, where Fat rented a cafe/hotel for his business and lived in one of the rooms. Cousin Fat drove fast, pretty cars. He knew how to make moonshine and sold it in the café. He also taught my dad how to make and sell it—which unfortunately led to Dad spending time in jail and prison for selling moonshine liquor. Fat's two-story building had a large dance area at the front entrance. As soon as the quarter dropped in the jukebox, the music filled the space, ears, and hearts of everyone in the room.

Athens is where Dad met my mom, Laura Crawford, and they married on July 17, 1944. Dad often talked about having applied for a job with the railroad, only to be turned down because he could not read. When Dad received a letter in the mail, he would call one of us to read the letter and explain it to him, and it was unacceptable to show any apprehension about reading or explaining the letter because we were going to school every day to be educated. If we did not understand something in the letter, we had to tell him that we would reread it for better understanding. We tried to avoid his piercing look and chiding comments about us "not knowing but going to school every day." At all costs, we wanted him to understand that we were being educated at the level of understanding we were capable of and trying to rise to his expectations.

Dad could not read but he could write his name, add and subtract numbers in his head, and was extremely accurate when counting money or receiving change from a purchase. He worked various day jobs to earn money and was an entrepreneur. Dad set up a business of digging graves in cemeteries. Rural cemeteries especially needed him, and funeral homes found out about him through word of mouth. He also opened up a small restaurant on Callaway Corner—a big accomplishment. This soul-food restaurant sold collard greens, cabbage, mac and cheese, fried chicken, pork chops, peas, candied yams, and cornbread. Later, he worked as a janitor at an elementary school.

Dad attended Little Creek Baptist Church in Greene County. The small membership meant that his church held services only two Sundays a month. One of our neighbors, also a member of Little Creek Baptist, encouraged my dad to attend service on a particular Sunday, which just happened to be the day we called "Homecoming," and Dad committed to being there. Homecoming allowed all former church members and friends to come back and fellowship, talk, eat, worship, and enjoy being together. Some would bring food to be arranged on a long table and eaten after the service. On the Saturday evening before Homecoming, Dad asked me to attend with him. I agreed, and we left our house early the next morning. The church was about twenty-five miles from Athens, but the car ride felt two hours long. Trying to stay awake, I knew when we were nearing the church because the car bounced violently when it left the pavement to follow the dirt road.

Almost there … a little farther down the road, on the left …

As Dad was getting out of the car, a person yelled out, "Hey, Abe!" Dad replied, "Hey, man!" They continued to greet each other with questions about how each was getting along, as well as questions about family. This went on for a while. As time passed, others came over and joined in, starting the greetings all over. Dad eventually got around to introducing me as his daughter, and I shyly smiled and said hello. Finally, we made our way inside the church, with ushers and others greeting my dad before we were seated. The gospel music sounded good, and those moved spiritually by the music stood up, clapped their hands, or said, "Amen." The sermon was long, and before church was over, a few members slipped outside to organize the food table, allowing the minister to bless the food before we were dismissed. I could feel love swirling all about from the time we arrived until the time we left!

Dad knew most Black men in Athens, and he always stopped and talked with people when they approached him. My dad accomplished a great deal with his personality, his hands-on learning ability, and his eagerness and desire to be a small-business owner. In later years, he helped one of my brothers pull out and replace a motor in his car, although he was not a mechanic. When one of us asked Dad how he was able to fix broken household equipment with no prior knowledge of the appliance, he would answer with his favorite reply: "Use the common sense that you have."

Listening to Dad's stories about his early childhood experiences gave us a deep appreciation of the difficulties of his upbringing, as well as the challenges he faced and how he overcame them early on. Although he worked well with his hands and learned how to repair things with logical thinking, Dad preached to us about the importance of going to school and getting a good education.

Very few excuses would justify missing a single day of school.

My mom was born and raised in Athens. She was an only child, raised by her grandmother in Linnentown. Mom attended high school and completed the eleventh grade. She was smart, so I'm not sure why she did not continue her education. Mom was seventeen years old when she married my dad, who was twenty-four. Mom would not ever admit to us how much Daddy's looks, his complexion, nice black hair, and bright smile played a role in her being attracted to him. She would simply smile and turn her head without a reply when we asked why she liked him.

By the time she turned twenty-six, she'd had seven children. My mom loved all of us, but she seemed to show favoritism to her sons. It was obvious to us girls because she'd cook what the boys requested, but when we asked for a particular dish, she'd point to the kitchen, and say, "Get started. I'll be in later." When we were all together talking, laughing, and eating, the subject of her sons being her favorites came up. She'd laugh as we teased her throughout the entire conversation, only to hear her insist, "I love you all equally."

She was also a disciplinarian when she thought we needed or deserved to be brought back in line for negative behaviors. When she demanded, "Go get a switch," the culpable one would start slowly moving toward the door, while the rest would freeze perfectly still. Going to get the switch was enough mental punishment, let alone being hit with it. Mom did not always get around to using it, which was a relief.

I'm sure we did not make it any easier on her; all seven of us were always so full of energy, needing her involvement to settle disputes. She'd often resort to getting Katie or Abe Jr.'s input before singling out the culprit. Katie knew exactly what had occurred between siblings. She'd often step in to restore calm by simply saying, "I don't remember." Abe Jr. also knew what had occurred and would reply, "I don't know." Katie was protective of her brothers and sisters, and she'd ask Mom if she could take the punishment instead. Sometimes her intervention worked, sometimes it didn't. However, when she was punished for something she had done, or on our behalf, she never cried. I always looked at her in amazement. I wasn't a crybaby, but anytime Mom started talking about punishing me for anything I'd done, tears would start flowing.

Dad was not a disciplinarian. He only stepped in when our brothers got into trouble, which was rarely. He talked to them sternly, instead of telling them, "Go get me a switch." His instructions were followed by, "Make haste." Our steps would quicken after hearing these words. When Dad was at home, his presence would always bring calm to the household. He repeatedly told us to use the common sense we had because it would get us through things we didn't quite understand. When he started repeating the "common sense" spiel, I slowly walked away, for I had not yet connected with my common sense. Hopefully, I would be able to do so sometime in the future.

Some mornings, we would wake up and start talking about whatever was on our minds, and, somehow, our conversations moved from talking to pillow fights, which we enjoyed. It was always girls against boys. We laughed and giggled endlessly until our daddy would interrupt with his loud, deep voice saying, "Cut it out!"—which brought everything to a sudden stop. If one of us was brave enough to continue, he would repeat himself: "I said cut it out, or I'm coming in there." None of us wanted that. We knew if he came in the room, he would come with belt in hand and threaten us with it. There was no such thing as "time out."

My mother was an excellent cook and worked at the school

cafeterias in her younger years. Being a cook at a school back in those days had its perks: cooks were allowed to carry home the leftover food. On most days, we looked forward to eating more of the food that we had eaten for lunch when we got home. This was a welcome treat for us and our friends who came by to eat. Spaghetti with meat sauce was a favorite, as were hot dogs with homemade rolls and strawberry shortcake. When Mom made yeast rolls, we'd stay close to home, waiting until she pulled them out of the oven, and our friends in the neighborhood came over to eat the rolls that "Mrs. Laura Maude" baked. The aroma from her rolls was mouthwatering even when she was just buttering them while they were rising on top of the stove. They were delicious! They would actually melt in your mouth. There was no such thing as getting just one or even two on a plate; five to six were eaten at a time. Yeast rolls with grape jelly or molasses syrup were the only food on our plates. Mom also made the best cinnamon rolls with raisins and white icing on top, and these were delicious as well.

Mom's homemade soup was the best. She would always start the soup with dried beans that she had soaked overnight as a base. She added fresh vegetables one by one, followed by basic seasoning. After that, she'd use all the leftover vegetables she had in the refrigerator. She'd pour the broth from a cooked chicken, as well as the thickening, which was made of water and flour, and season to taste. It was the best soup. She was an excellent cook, and could make a meal out of whatever she had in the kitchen.

I was very tall for my age and extremely sensitive. Being the middle child (fourth out of seven), it was easy for me to walk in the shadow of my siblings. As a result, I was often overlooked, left alone, and seemed invisible. I was extremely shy, and it was challenging for me to vocalize my feelings and defend myself. Perhaps because my siblings also knew I was the quiet one, they pushed me around and easily embarrassed me.

Besides music, I enjoyed TV. My Aunt Bessie and Uncle Dave had a TV set, but we did not. They had no children, and my sister Pete lived with them from a very young age, so we were in and out of their house a lot. Most evenings, we'd be sprawled on their living room floor, watching shows like *The Ed Sullivan Show*, *Gunsmoke*, and others. Pete enjoyed watching movies. Each day at noon, a movie was featured on *Armchair Playhouse*. I sometimes joined her, and we watched whatever movie was on.

For years, I kept to myself and vicariously lived through my adventurous and social siblings, especially Katie. However, once I started attending middle school, I thoroughly enjoyed academics and my personality evolved into being a social butterfly. My favorite teachers were Miss Susie Mattie Hawkins, my fourth-grade teacher, and Miss Wilhelmina Hardeman, my fifth-grade teacher. Both truly encouraged my academic growth. They paid special attention to me and encouraged my learning. As a result, I really tried to work harder on my schoolwork for them. My favorite subject at that time was English, and I took an interest in Chorus and being a majorette.

At school one day, an announcement came over the intercom, inviting any third- to sixth-grade girls wishing to be majorette to meet in the lunchroom after school that coming Friday. After gathering, we were lined up by height and directed to march between and around tables while listening to music playing over the intercom. All the girls tried hard to be in step with the music while the teachers looked over the group for possible selection.

After a week of practicing after school, majorette selection was made the following Friday. We assembled in the lunchroom after school and were directed to sit on each side of long lunchroom tables. The teachers came in, and a couple talked about how much they appreciated all of us trying out, but only a few would be selected. Then another teacher started calling names of those who had been selected. After hearing a few names, I held my breath nervously. It was only after hearing my name that I started breathing again. I was so happy! I wanted to be a marching majorette. I had no idea what the majorettes did, but I wanted to be chosen. This was my first competition in anything. Wow! I felt very good about myself.

My friend Evelyn, however, was not chosen. Evelyn lived in Linnentown and was a year older than me. We played together after school. The day of the majorette selection, I was riding home from practice with her and her dad. Evelyn had started crying in the lunchroom after she realized she had not been selected, was still crying when her father picked us up, and continued to cry the entire ride home. For days, at school and afterward, she was sad and cried when she thought about not being a majorette. After a few days had passed, she appeared to be herself again as we played. She said, "I'm going to be a majorette, because my mom told me so." We were both happy, and eventually Evelyn did become a majorette.

At school, our majorette leader told us we were going to have outfits made for us by Mrs. Williams, who lived on Rocksprings Street. She pulled out a pattern and materials. The materials were very pretty white and green satin, which made us feel special. After I made two trips to Mrs. Williams's house for sizing, my outfit was a perfect fit. To our delight, we learned we would be marching in Athens' yearly Christmas parade, so we practiced hard and learned a few steps to perform on signal.

We gathered in a designated location before the parade started, admiring each other in our beautiful green-and-white uniforms. I remember looking over at Evelyn after we had lined up. She looked so happy. I looked around and saw that we all looked pretty and cheerful. We marched and stopped and performed on signal. So many people lined both sides of the streets, and they clapped enthusiastically as we walked by. It was a long walk, but we marched with pride. This was the only time I can remember us wearing those majorette uniforms, but that experience made us feel special for many years.

It was through my friendship with Evelyn that I was introduced to the National Association for the Advancement of Colored People (NAACP). I was invited to attend NAACP meetings with Evelyn and her older sister, and I was very intrigued. This was my first experience attending an organized meeting of any kind. Our leader was Mr. Red Weaver, whose talks focused on equality, integration, and how our future could be different if we'd get involved to help lead the effort for changes needed in our city and country. Once I had started attending meetings regularly, Mr. Weaver asked my parents if they'd allow me to join, and they agreed. I became very active. There was a president, a secretary taking minutes, and voting rules that were all new to me. I soon learned parliamentary procedure. After meetings, Mr. Weaver sometimes drove us home.

A district meeting in Augusta, Georgia, was scheduled for that summer, and Mr. Weaver wanted us to attend. I planned to go but did not have anything to wear. Katie had a new gold skirt and a white blouse. She had not yet worn it herself, but she wanted me to wear her new outfit to this meeting. I was so happy about her display of such unselfish behavior; her actions communicated how much she loved me. Mr. Weaver drove us to the church in Augusta, where the district meeting was being held. It was a big church, and people were walking, standing, and talking as we neared the church's vicinity.

Wow! I thought. *This place is filled with young people like me!*

During the meeting, I was so impressed with how some speakers were addressing the attendees. They appeared to be my age, and they spoke so eloquently about integration and the changes we needed in our country. We were there all day listening to different speakers, and did not get back home until late that night. I was delighted to have attended.

NAACP meetings inspired me to become involved in the Civil Rights movement when I was fourteen years old. I was a member of Ebenezer Baptist Church West, about a three-mile walk from my home, and I walked to the church each morning. Rev. William J. Hudson was my pastor at that time and was one of the main leaders of the movement in Athens. He was a fearless man who did not back away and was very direct in his conversation with us and other community leaders who approached him.

The following summer of 1962, a young man named Bobby Hill became our new leader. Athens was his hometown, and he was either home from college or about to start law school. He gave us directions for sit-ins and marches in downtown Athens. The local students who were involved the previous year returned, except those who had left for college and those expected to get a job. There were some new faces, those who had not been old enough to participate the previous year but were now mature enough to help the cause.

The church was our meeting place, or "headquarters," as we

referred to it. We talked about using nonviolent behavior, regardless of the situation we found ourselves in. We talked about what we could expect when we walked into a hostile environment. Our leaders decided that our focus of demonstration would be marching and engaging in sit-ins in downtown Athens. We were determined to integrate the city.

Downtown Athens had department stores that didn't allow Black customers to walk through the front entrance to shop—we had to use the back doors. After entering the stores, while going up the elevator or walking to the retail area, it was an unspoken rule that a Black shopper would be the last person to be assisted for anything. The five-and-dime stores that had lunch counters did not serve Blacks, and their two water fountains were segregated by signs reading "Colored" and "White." Living in the South, especially in the city of Athens and Linnentown, had well prepared me for discriminatory behaviors, and we demanded fair treatment.

Being an active member of NAACP at an early age prepared me as well. We discussed appropriate dress and what to expect if we were sent to jail. Demonstrations continued for hours at a time each day and each week. We knew when we were going to be arrested: the police would start directing us to yellow school buses and told to get in. We younger ones were taken to the stockade and dropped off. We were locked inside the fence until nightfall, without food or water. The older kids were taken downtown to jail, charged, and held until they were released on bail.

When we were all released, cars were waiting to carry us back to the church. We sang and listened to inspirational messages delivered mostly by a visiting pastor each night. I remember the audience singing the powerful hymn "We Shall Overcome" every night while linking hands. From church, we were picked up by our parents or walked home. The next day we would return and repeat the cycle.

Each day, once we got to the Ebenezer church, we made protest signs and chatted before being divided into groups. Some would just demonstrate with signs, while others would be involved in sit-ins at the lunch counters. Our transportation would drop us off near the First United Methodist Church on North Lumpkin. Several times we were involved in sit-ins at lunch counters at the five-and-dime stores, a drug store, and the downtown Varsity restaurant. From the moment we unloaded from cars that dropped us off, I felt my muscles stiffen as I walked along those threatening paths. My stomach would tighten with every step I took, as I was well aware of what was waiting to unfold as I turned left on the corner of Clayton and Lumpkin. Both edges of the sidewalk would be lined with White men and women shouting the N-word mixed with profanity, and women used their purses as weapons, hitting us as we walked by.

The sidewalks between the front of the stores and the parking meters did not allow for much space. The White agitators standing and yelling on both sides didn't leave us much room for walking. When we reached our assigned store, we sat very quietly at the lunch counter. If we faced the cooking area, our backs were to the crowds and we did not look back. The name-calling and cussing took place, but we did not see facial expressions, which was just as nerve-racking. We sat through this for hours, and then on a cue, quietly got up and left. This was repeated each day and each week.

I was in the group demonstrating with signs for hours. It was exhausting. I would walk and look down while holding my sign, being careful not to bump the person in front of me. We walked to the end of the block, turned, and walked back. The White people's anger was so palpable that I was scared to look up as I walked. On the rare occasion I did, I could see the anger in the faces of the men and women. These were the men and women who thought they were speaking for Athens: "No integration here!" But I knew better because other White women and men joined us at our nightly meetings at Ebenezer and supported the Civil Rights cause.

One evening before leaving church, we learned that we would be demonstrating in front of the Varsity near the church on Broad Street the next evening. We needed to come prepared to stay late into the evening. The Varsity was just a block away, so we would walk. The following evening, after we had assembled in the church pews, the reverend announced that the Ku Klux Klan would be marching on the sidewalk on the opposite site of the Varsity. We sat in the church until we were asked to line up in single file, which was our normal routine. The line slowly moved out the front entrance, down the steps onto the sidewalk, and then continued to Broad Street. I could hear car horns blowing and loud shouts before we reached Broad. The traffic in both lanes were backed up.

As we walked further, I caught a glimpse of what all the commotion was about: two large men had white hoods on their heads with white flowing cloaks. Moving from Chase Street to Broad, I had a full view of about twelve to fifteen (what appeared to be men) with the same white hoods on their heads. I was aware that the Klan wore hoods from listening to older adults and watching movies on TV, but I never anticipated being this close to a Klansman dressed in their scary outfits. I was so intimidated looking at them. Even though we had prepared to see the Klan, their dress, the traffic, noise, and police officers overwhelmed me. The traffic was moving slowly as they drove by, blowing their car horns in support of them while shouting obscenities at us. Our leaders were close by, which gave me comfort. When our leaders told us it was time to go, I was so relieved to walk back to the church. It was certainly a memorable evening.

On the walk home that night, I thought about food. Most days, the last meal I had eaten was breakfast. I could not wait to get home to eat, for I knew Mom had brought food home or she had prepared a meal after work with whatever food was in the kitchen. I often thought, while walking home, about the women who lined either side of the sidewalks with their husbands or boyfriends. My young mind could not fathom how women could curse and be so mean to children. I knew that the majority had their own children or nieces and nephews. Were they just following the crowd, or were they naturally mean people?

Chapter Two
COMMUNITY LIFE IN LINNENTOWN

L iving in a community with so many family members had advantages: it gave my parents and others the opportunity for everyone to support each other. My dad moved his paternal grandparents, Katie and Jim Thomas, from Greene County, Georgia, to a vacant house on S. Finley Street. Dad said they were getting older, and he needed to frequently check on them. I had visited them a number of times at their home in Greene County, where I had also participated in Homecoming family gatherings at Little Creek Baptist Church. My great-grandmother wore an apron that covered the front of her dress and was talkative, while my great-grandfather hardly said anything. He was truly a man of very few words.

They both adjusted after moving to Athens. My great-grandparents welcomed another grandson, Fred L. Thomas, into their home during the summer months. Fred L., as we called him, was attending Floyd T. Curry High School in Greene County. When my great-grandparents moved to Linnentown, Fred L. continued to live in Greene County to finish high school, but in the summer months, he'd come to Athens to work so he could purchase school clothing for the following year. Fred L. asked our cousin Freddie Mae to select clothing for him. He returned the favor by selling her a 45-inch rhythm & blues record for one dollar. What a win-win for both!

My mother's grandmother, the one we called "Ma Minnie," lived next door to us. She raised my mother and her daughter, my Aunt Lila Mae. Ma Minnie was very short, heavy, and her walking was always unsteady. She had the responsibility of keeping us children during the day when we weren't in school, while my mother, dad, and Aunt Lila Mae worked. As years passed, Lila Mae had about seven children, and there were also seven of us. Not only did Ma Minnie keep all fourteen of us great-grandkids, she had the responsibility of cooking for us and our parents.

Ma Minnie had big straw rocking chairs in the front room and on her front porch. She would put us down for naps every day, keeping all of us in one room to keep an eye on us as we slept. She'd put as many of us in the bed as possible and make pallets of quilts and spreads on the floor for the rest. If one of us was fussy, she would pick that child up, sit in her rocking chair, and rock that child back to sleep.

After we awakened, we usually ate hot dogs and pork & beans. All fourteen of us ate off heavy plastic plates, as we had no money for paper plates or cups. About this time, we could smell what she had started cooking for supper. She cooked dried peas or beans every single day. Pinto beans, black-eyed peas, butter beans, white beans—and then started the cycle over. Every morning, we had homemade biscuits with grits. Rarely did we have sausage or bacon, which was a treat, and when we did, we were only permitted to have one piece. We spread molasses syrup on biscuits. I ate so much of it in the past that the smell of it today causes my nose discomfort.

My great-grandmother Ma Minnie wasn't the only family member who lived near us. Two houses stood near the backyard of our house, and my grandmother Ma Mat lived in one. We referred to them as "shotgun" houses because it was said that they were so small, a bullet shot from the front door would pass through the house without hitting anything and exit through the back door. These houses had a "front room," which was used as a living room or bedroom, a "middle room," which was also used as a bedroom, and a kitchen. The kitchens had wood-burning stoves and ice boxes. These houses had no electricity, so kerosene lamps were used at night for lighting and one small fireplace heated the entire house. They had front and back doors and an enclosed commode on the back porch. The rental houses were about sixteen feet wide with front porches and tin roofs. There was not much distance between the houses, and they were aligned along a downward slope to allow a good view from the first to the last house.

The wood on the outside of the house looked like pine, but it was hard to determine. None of the rentals had an ounce of paint on them. The landlord only collected rent; she did not repair, replace, or paint anything. The houses did have front porches, where we all spent some idle time. I loved lying in bed, listening to the rain hit the tin roof. It had a soothing effect at night and in the early morning hours. In the summertime, rain and high humidity resulted in unbearable heat inside. We had no air conditioning, only floor fans. When thunderstorms occurred, it sometimes sounded as if the storm was right on top of our roof. It was frightening and always kept me awake. When the rain stopped, it was a relief to move from inside to the front porch, where it was cooler.

Aunt Bessie and Uncle Dave also lived across the street, and a great-aunt lived on Lyndon Row. Aunt Bessie's house was made with wood and what looked like asphalt siding, the front porch was made of cement and had a screen door that opened to the outside, and there were steps from the street to their front yard. She took good care of us when Mom and Dad weren't around. Uncle Dave worked at a fraternity house on the UGA campus and walked there each every day. Aunt Bessie worked as a housekeeper at a home in the Five Points area. She and some other women working in that same area hired a taxi driver to take them to and from work each day.

Aunt Bessie always had hot dogs in her refrigerator, and we ate lunch at her house on countless summer days. Sometimes at my house, we happily ate folded sandwich bread with catsup and mustard, but no hot dogs. Another treat was eating corn flakes, when my parents could afford a box. Someone would yell, "We're having cereal for breakfast!" and we all reacted by jumping out of bed. Filling seven bowls, one box lasted only a few minutes. A can of evaporated milk was used instead of whole milk when we ate corn flakes. We prepared the milk by pouring the 12-ounce can into a pitcher, adding 12 ounces of water, sugar to taste, and a little vanilla. We all smiled contentedly while eating.

My cousin Freddie Mae, an only child, lived on Lyndon Row. My family thought she was rich because her parents owned two houses in the community. Both of Freddie Mae's parents worked at UGA. Her mother, Mrs. Susie Mae, walked down Lyndon Row to Cloverhurst every day to get to her housekeeping job in the Home Economics building. After crossing Cloverhurst, her shortcut included a steep embankment, and getting down it without falling was a major challenge.

One morning, she was surprised to see steps cut into the hill. Sometime later, the family learned that Mrs. Susie Mae's brother-in-law Wayne, who everyone called "Horse," had cut out the steps in the steep hill so she could walk down to a flat landing without falling. After hearing Mrs. Susie Mae talking with family members about the difficulty she was having walking down this hill every morning, Wayne, who had limited mobility as well as a speech and hearing impairment, took matters into his own hands, without being asked and without telling anyone.

Although we lived in a small house, Dad extended an invitation to my aunt, her two daughters, and their children to live with us for a short period of time. We all had to make adjustments with the additional family members. I was aware of other family members in Linnentown with mother, children, and grandmother living together, and this was also true of friends at school. Families in the community always helped their own.

No matter the circumstances, the people of Linnentown supported each other. I also remember Mrs. Jababe's husband, Mr. Shepmore, who had gotten pretty sick and was bedridden. Mrs. Jababe told my mother that she needed a helping hand, as she had to carry everything to her husband's bedside to take care of him. She asked Mom if she'd allow one of her children to assist for a short period of time. I guess she asked my mother because there were seven children. Mom told me to go to her house and stay for a while just to help her out, because she was old.

Why me? I asked myself (but not to my mom). I just did not want to leave home. I was about nine years old—what could I do to help Mrs. Jababe? Granted, it was just a few doors up and across the street, but leaving home to stay with someone else was like going to a different part of the city. I didn't know them personally; just saying hello at a distance was all I had done. They had no children, so I had never been inside their home.

I was very uncomfortable going to their house, but Mom had already decided for me. I did not carry any clothes with me because I was told to come home every morning and return to their house every evening. When I first went to Mrs. Jababe's house, she showed me a small twin bed that I would be sleeping in, the bathroom, living room, and small TV. I had no one to play with there. I do remember her buying me a small dollhouse with furniture inside. The first few nights there, I was going back and forth from her husband's room to the kitchen, taking him glasses of water. He would always tell me, "God is going to bless you," as I was walking back to the kitchen with his empty glass. No other words were exchanged between us. He died shortly after my arrival. I was not sad about his death, as I did not really know him. I just wanted to be back at home.

Other men in the neighborhood also worked with their hands. When someone in our neighborhood needed a plumber or electrician, they would reach out to a neighbor who had the skill to repair what was broken. After the repair had been made, no money was exchanged; payment had to wait until Friday, pay day. Oftentimes, the person making the repair knew the family's situation and wouldn't take any money. A "thank you" was enough.

Women in the neighborhood got together to make lye soap. I don't know exactly how they made it, but I stood watching from start to finish. It appeared that someone always brought what they needed to put in the large black pot set over a fire. The women's conversations, which lasted throughout the process, revolved around how everybody was doing in the community and about their jobs. Once the soap was made, they cut it up into cakes and divided them up, taking some to other neighbors. Every type of cleaning was done with this multipurpose soap: washing dishes, scrubbing floors, washing hands, and bathing. In the summertime, my mom and Aunt Lila Mae would make a fire under a large black pot of water. When the water was hot, she would fill a large wash tub, then bathe us one by one in the tub. I'm not sure how clean the child was who got the last bath!

In Linnentown, the front porch was used to communicate with all neighbors passing by. "Hello" and "How are you doing?" would often lead to long conversations about who was sick in the neighborhood or a bit of gossip. On one particular day, I overheard what was being shared about a middle-aged single woman in our neighborhood. She had decided she wanted to get married, so she had filled out paperwork to order a husband from a veteran's retirement home. She had described the qualities she wanted in him, and if he did not have these qualities once he arrived, she did not have to keep him; she could send him back. The husband-to-be was set to come in the next month or so. Other women in the community did not understand why she would go through this much trouble to marry someone she did not know. It did not make sense to them. As I was listening, I thought, *Why doesn't this make sense? She should be able to send him back if he's not what she wants.* I was really at a disadvantage, for I was eavesdropping, couldn't ask questions, and should not have been listening anyway.

At that point, another neighbor walked up, and the conversation immediately changed. She shared information about a male neighbor down the street. His wife and children had moved out, and he had been alone for a couple of months. While sitting on her front porch one day, she had observed him walking from around the back of his house with another woman. They were slowly walking to his car parked on the street in front of his house. He waved and said hello.

"Well, the woman looked in my direction and did not speak, just turned her head, and looked up," the neighbor said. "She was acting very saditty, if you ask me." ("Saditty" was a word Black people often used when referring to snobbish or arrogant people.)

Another neighbor asked, "What happened between him and his wife?"

"Nobody knows," replied two women, shrugging.

Suddenly, we heard a voice from the group yell out, "Y'all children go out in the yard and play!" That ended my eavesdropping on our neighbors' gossiping. Off to play we went.

Mr. Ervin and Mrs. Ida's house on Lyndon Row was the gathering place for the adults. Mr. Ervin loved putting a card table at the edge of the yard every evening and hosting a card game of Spades, or "pitty pat," as we called it. There were always two to four neighbors playing cards and two to four waiting to play.

I watched the adults play this card game. They shuffled the deck of cards, turned the top card over, then dealt each person five cards. If there were pairs in a player's hand, the player would remove those cards and place them on the table. The player could pull a card from the deck or use a card thrown out by another player. The object of pitty pat was to be the first player to get rid of all your cards by forming them into pairs.

Mr. Ervin was so dramatic when he thought he had a winning hand, or when he thought his team would win. He would stand up from the table and slam each card down when it was his turn to play, all while talking trash to the opposing team. Still standing while the cards were being shuffled, he'd say, "Y'all can't play cards! This game is over! Who's next?" Other players would holler, "Man, sit down! Sit down and shut up, so we can play and finish this game!" Mr. Ervin would finally sit down, still talking trash.

I remember another time stopping near the card table, listening to the players talk about Mr. William L. "Babe" Davis while playing cards. They were recalling his talented abilities—"best left-fielder who ever played in the Negro League"—as they spoke and agreed simultaneously. "And there was not another player who could touch his skill level."

Mr. Davis had played with the Atlanta Black Crackers. I had heard others talk about his greatness when he played professional baseball. He lived on Finley in the rental houses with his family. Everyone who knew of his athletic abilities proudly shared his performance and contributions to baseball during his playing years, 1937–1939. He was Christine Davis Johnson's uncle. As a child, she remembers trips with her family to watch him play at a stadium on Ponce de Leon in Atlanta.

Mariah "Pus" Jackson was born in 1861 in Athens, Georgia. She was my and Freddie Mae's great-grandmother. Mariah lived at 181 Lyndon Row in Linnentown in the 1930s, according to the WPA Slave Narratives Interviews Project. Her name was changed in the interview to "Cindy Wright" to protect her privacy and safety. The narrative was her personal story set in December 1938 and written in her dialect.

Mariah was a midwife in Athens and checked on her patients about a week after delivery. I looked at my mother's birth certificate and was stunned to learn that Mariah had delivered her, and that she was living on Lyndon Row at the time. Wow! It was absolutely amazing to see her name on my mom's birth's certificate, dated June 21, 1927. Mariah was married and had given birth to fourteen children. She died on December 20, 1938, shortly after she was interviewed. The interviewer attended her funeral and the order of her funeral service was fully documented. This is the only written documentation we have of any relative from Mariah's generation.

While the majority of houses on Lyndon Row had hedges in the front yards separating them from the dirt road, some had beautiful lawns behind the hedges. Mrs. Ida had the prettiest yard on Lyndon Row. Cement blocks separated her yard from the dirt road, and on both sides of the walkway leading to her house were big, beautiful, green elephant-ear plants of all different sizes. Her entire front yard was filled with all different types and sizes of greenery.

One day, as I walked up Mrs. Ida's sidewalk, I noticed that some of her elephant-ear plants were taller than me! They were so green. They looked as if she had polished them with furniture polish. I observed her watering the plants early in the mornings with a hose she kept in her yard. She examined each one as she watered it. Her plants were so tall that you couldn't see her front porch from the street. What pride she took in her plants!

I developed my love for tulips as I admired the yard of Mrs. Jababe each year. Both sides of her walkway were lined with beautiful tulips of different colors leading to her front porch. From the street, her block house—the only one on Finley—looked very pretty with her tulips blooming in her front yard.

Linnentown residents grew not only flowers but also food on

their property. Mrs. Nellie Hunter raised chickens directly beside her house. The enclosed chicken pen and coop area were about six steps down from her kitchen door. She kept fresh eggs on her kitchen table in a wire bowl and would sell them to neighbors. She was also in charge of the yearly Easter egg hunt. The entire neighborhood, adults and children, would gather at the Legion Pool field (and later at another field in the community) for the big egg hunt. Each family sent a dozen beautifully decorated eggs that had been dipped in bold and vibrant-colored dyes. Some had beautiful stickers, and others had designs made with a clear wax crayon pencil. The adults and older children hid the eggs, while we younger children waited elsewhere in our Easter outfits, holding our baskets. Once Mrs. Nellie gave the ready signal, we all raced to designated locations according to our age group. One child in each age group who found the most eggs got a prize. Chocolate eggs were also hidden and finding them was an extra treat. The prizes were awarded after the egg hunt.

Besides flowers and chickens, trees were important in our community for beauty and fruit. Mrs. Nellie had a huge magnolia tree at the edge of her front yard. The height and width of this tree were enormous, and it produced gigantic white flowers with large green leaves. The flowers and leaves were so big and pretty. I would sometimes break one off, take it home, and put it in a jar with water. These flowers had a lemony smell and were my first experience detecting a fragrance from a flower. The smell reminded me of the lemon extract my mother used when baking. Playing with the flower petals, talking to them, and smelling them turned the white petals yellowish, then brown. I always threw away the ones I played with the following day and went back to the tree for a fresh one.

One day, I decided to break off two instead of one. After putting both flowers in the jar of water, I stepped back when the jar turned over and fell to the floor. The flowers were too heavy for the jar. After mopping up the water and throwing out the broken flowers, I decided that in the future, I would only pick one flower at a time.

However, we could not pick pears from Mrs. Susie's pear tree on a lot she owned across the street, so we took what we wanted at dusk. We were not sure why she would not give us pears from her tree, especially after we asked her so politely if we could have a few. We just assumed that she didn't like children. The pears were falling off the tree, but she was not picking them up, either from the tree or off the ground. Periodically, she would send her husband, Mr. Mitchell, to pick some to bring back to her.

Some of us kids would talk one of my brothers, either Abe or Pepper, into climbing up in the tree to shake it. When Mrs. Susie realized we were shaking the tree, she would holler, "Get out of my pear tree and stop shaking it! Y'all children are stealing my pears! Y'all should be ashamed of yourselves!"

Hearing her yelling would put a stop to the tree-shaking, and my brother would come down from the tree. We picked up as many pears as we could carry and started running and laughing in the opposite direction, the sound of her voice slowly fading. When we reached Peabody, we stopped running and sat on the street curb to eat the pears. They were delicious.

Mrs. Gertrude Clarke lived on Lyndon Row. She was petite, less than five feet tall in height and extra small in size. She was very dedicated to her church, Ebenezer Baptist Church West, the same church I attended. She invited children to her house on Wednesday evenings for Bible study. It didn't matter how many attended—even if I was the only child there, we prayed, sang, and had Bible study. I attended because she always served the best homemade cookies afterwards. The younger children knew if we showed her our report card from school, she would review it and encourage us, regardless if it was good or not so good. Afterward, she would give each child a dime.

Although everyone got along with each other and life was good, living in Linnentown had some stressful moments. Residents experienced many headaches, especially from living in close proximity to the UGA campus. Our community was often the target of negative and unwanted behavior. I distinctively remember students driving through Linnentown and throwing soda bottles, cans, or cups from their cars at us. The cars slowly drove down the street, with their windows down. Right before passing, one or two students would hurl items through the windows, and the driver would then speed off with passengers looking back, laughing. Sometimes we could anticipate where the bottles and cans would land so we could avoid being hit, but other times we were not so fortunate.

When there were home football games, our community was invaded by fans looking for places to park their cars. Some had arrogant attitudes and parked with no hesitancy in front of home-owners' driveways, which prevented residents from getting their cars in or out of their own driveways. This caused major frustrations. Fans also drove their cars onto our front yards, without receiving any permission from homeowners. To prevent a possibility confrontation with a fan, or an accident occurring to a car, children were told to "car sit" until the football fans returned. Car sitting meant that we had to sit and watch the cars to make sure no damage happened to the cars because our parents didn't want any trouble. They didn't want to be wrongly accused of damage or a stolen car.

Game day also brought a great deal of litter, as fans repeatedly threw trash in our yards. An unspoken expectation, we had to pick up all trash that was either brought back from the game or tossed from cars.

As if having bottles being thrown at us was not enough, we also had to deal with all the mud that seemed to be everywhere because of the unpaved streets. Mud filled in every crevice whenever it rained. If we were out of school when it started raining, we would stand on the front porch and watch the cars swerving back and forth in the mud. Sometimes, a car would swerve out of control, and one or two tires would land in a ditch. The tires would spin and spin, splashing mud all over the car and on anyone who was within yards of it. When this happened, we'd start giggling and laughing while pointing at the car, for we had seen this happen many times, watching in anticipation of when the driver would be getting out to assess his situation.

One time, when a driver finally stopped the car and reluctantly stepped out into the tire-deep mud grooves, he attempted to walk to the other side of the car by firmly placing and moving his hand along the car to steady himself, all the while looking down at his shoes. Were they being sucked into the mud? We watched closer in anticipation. The driver inevitably stopped and stared at the car tires for a long time, as if asking himself, *How in the hell am I going to get this car out of the mud?!*

A neighbor walked up and interrupted his staring by asking, "Do you need help?" A conversation started between the two men as other neighbors just showed up with planks in hand to put under the stuck tires. The driver was asked to get back in his car, while three or four men put planks under the tires as they pushed. The minute the tires caught traction, the car shot out of the mud.

The driver simply threw up his hand as he drove off, signaling thank you, leaving behind the mud-covered men. This happened often, and the men in our neighborhood always showed up to assist without being asked to do so and without being paid, providing unspoken support only the neighbors knew. This was entertainment for us children on rainy days, when we could not play outside because of the weather.

After a few days of rain, it was almost impossible to walk across the street without a shoe getting sucked into the mud. It could happen in the middle of the road or near the edge. You knew it was happening when your foot was moving and the mud was sucking down your shoe. You'd try to jerk on your shoe, but your bare foot would pop up. If there were no cars approaching, you could easily turn around to pick up your shoe. If a car was approaching, though, there was no option but to move out of the street far enough back to avoid mud splashes. It was crucial to never lose your shoe's location while the car passed, so that once the car was gone, you could retrieve the shoe without having to search for it in the mud. Then we would take the muddy shoe to the outside water faucet and clean it with running water, in hopes it would be somewhat dry the following morning—unless you wanted a shoe sopping wet!

There was never a good enough explanation to a parent about a lost shoe, since there was no money for buying new shoes. More often than not, we only had one pair. We all knew that shoes were purchased before the start of school and at Christmas. Walking in mud in the summertime was not such a big issue with us children because we were barefoot the majority of the time. We only had to rinse our feet at the outside faucets before entering our houses.

Tracking mud into the houses was another concern.

Sweeping and mopping were never-ending when it rained, especially for a long period of time. Getting off the school bus and walking in the mud to Ma Minnie's house was an adventure. When we reached the front porch, she'd open the screen door, standing with it ajar and stopping us with instructions to leave our shoes outside. The ten of us grandchildren knew the drill, but she would tell us anyway. She always instructed us firmly but kindly. When it was time for my siblings and me to go home, of course some mud would be tracked in from our socks or whatever we had dropped and picked up while walking to her house. At times, we were filthy with mud from our heads down to our feet.

Every once in a while, a street scraper would come to the community to scrape the unpaved streets. This was done by an operator driving a tractor with a flat 3' x 6' piece of steel attached to the front. The operator lowered the scraper into the dirt about two inches, then pushed it forward about two feet, over and over again, until both unpaved streets were completely level. We would follow behind the tractor, looking at the steel scraper's every move from start until finish. At the end, the streets were level and looked good, but all the dirt that had been pushed forward ended up on the very edges of the streets, blocking driveways of those who had cars, and others' front yards.

We often heard, "Well, damn, now I have to shovel the dirt from the yard and driveway," as a disgusted neighbor came with shovel and rake in hand to move dirt back into the street. When other adults got home later that day, profanity was directed at the scraper, long after it had gone.

The grown-ups continued to shake their heads in disgust and let out a bit more profanity. We would hear, "These streets need to be paved, not scraped!" and "Dammit, we pay taxes!" as another upset neighbor approached his driveway with a shovel. Soon enough, the dirt would be pressed down into the street, and the street scraper would come back to repeat the cycle.

Despite the aggravation of the unpaved streets, Linnentown residents took pride in their neighborhood. Rental houses were on one side of Finley, and on the other side lived proud homeowners who took care of their houses and property. None of the rentals had a blade of grass in the yards, so we had to use a brush broom to sweep them clean. It was the children's job to sweep the yards, and sweep them we did, especially in the summers.

Chapter Three
THE MOMENT
EVERYTHING CHANGED

A lthough family and community life seemed to be good in Linnentown, life as we knew it was about to change when we had to move out of our rental house. From that moment on, everything seemed to be on a downward spiral. Mrs. Doolittle, our White landlord, told my mom and dad the property had been sold and gave them a move date in the early part of 1958. At that time, none of the adults knew why the property had been sold.

Initially, families living in the rental houses were in shock. However, after the shock wore off, the urgency of searching for a house or a place to move began. Extra money was needed to move. Rent and utility deposits were a big challenge. Where would the money come from? Loans from extended family, an employer, or pulling a few dollars from weekly pay? How do you take money that is already designated for the bare essentials? Do you purchase fewer groceries or pay the least amount acceptable on bills?

There hadn't been too much turnover in Linnentown. Once a family moved here, they usually stayed for years or generations. We were living in a time when Blacks could only move to Black communities, and there were only so many in Athens. Being in this situation exasperated and worried my parents, particularly when there was a deadline for so many families to move out within the given timeframe. My dad and mom had to make a quick decision: Where do we relocate to?

It usually took years to acquire enough money for a down payment on an existing house. My parents' wages averaged about eighteen dollars a week. In previous years, the wages were even lower. This is why it took such a long time to save enough money to purchase property or save for a down payment for a house. Meager wages, plus the weekly expenses to care for one's family, left very little for anything else. Some families had anywhere from seven to nine children to feed each week. This was first and, sometimes, the only priority, while other bills were put on hold until the next payday.

Among those families who had to leave Finley Street, only a few had the money to buy a house. Others were making plans to move after purchasing lots in other areas of the city. The Finley Street residents' choices were limited to renting another house or apartment, renting a room by the week, moving in with family, or, as a last resort, moving to public housing.

My parents loved living in our community and wanted to stay. They were surrounded by the support needed from family and friends, which was especially helpful with seven small children. There were no vacant houses in Linnentown, so how would it be possible to stay?

Finally, our parents broke the news that they would buy a lot on Peabody and build a house. My mom was all smiles when she shared this news with us kids and her friends. To buy a lot and build a house in such a short period of time was unheard of and beyond any stretch of our imaginations. I was in elementary school at this time, and the thought of someone building a house in my community had never occurred to me. The houses were already there. Who would want to build a house in this day and in our community? Abe and Laura Maude Thomas, of course!

My mind was finally able to grasp the vision my parents had. Dad told Mom that he was going to build her a house, and he would reach out to men in our community to build it. Wow! All the skills needed to build a house were already in our community. My dad initially reached out to Mr. James ("Chill") Edward Brown for his assistance in building our home. Mr. Chill was a short man, about five feet tall, and very slim. Like my great-grandfather, he was not a man of many words, and he always had a pencil behind his ear. His skills were equal to those of an architect, and he was very smart.

Back in the late 1950s, the *Athens Banner Herald* highlighted new house styles, layouts included, in the magazine section of the Sunday paper. Dad asked Mom to pick a house that she liked. After a few Sundays had passed, my mother saw her dream house. It was a pretty big house compared to the three rooms we were currently living in. The new house had seven rooms: three bedrooms, living room, dining room, kitchen, and bath. Mom cut this picture from the paper while we children sat at the table with her. We loved the picture of the house and looked at her in sheer amazement when she told us this was all Mr. Chill needed to build our house.

Dad shared the picture with Mr. Chill and found out what materials he would need. Dad and Mr. Chill applied and received a building permit and were told the water and sewage on Peabody had been approved and would be installed by the time the house was completed. Afterward, they put a plan of action together as they sat on Mr. Chill's front porch. This plan included Dad contacting all the men in the community who had the required construction skills, acquiring the permit and the materials needed, deciding on a start date for the build, and determining the approximate completion date.

I remember standing in the driveway one day, watching Mr. Chill walk from the backyard with workers in tow. Just as they reached the now-framed house, Mr. Chill started giving instructions. The men from the community whom my father and Mr. Chill hired to build our house were asking him questions, and he was answering and giving directions. Dad had made several trips to an office in City Hall inquiring about the water and sewage lines installation, and the employee working in the office there gave him the same reply each time: "We are working on it."

This really upset Mom, for we needed to move when the house was ready, but how could we live there without water? Dad said that all money had been spent on construction. Our house was nearing completion and we had to move from Finley! A couple more weeks were estimated for completion. Why would the city issue a building permit, knowing that water and sewage would not be installed, and knowing this community had been approved for an urban renewal project? This was totally absurd and cold-hearted. My parents had depleted all the money they had saved to build the new home. They would not have purchased a lot if they had known our community had been approved for an urban renewal project.

Dad and Mr. Chill reasoned the water and sewage lines likely might not be installed, contrary to what they been told by the city. So what was the alternative? Dad asked our new neighbors, Mr. John and Julia Griffith, who had a water hydrant in the back of their house, if he could tie into their water line if he paid the water bill. Our neighbors agreed. Dad's focus turned to digging a ditch from the hydrant to outside our kitchen. From there the plumbing would be piped to the kitchen sink.

One day, Mom stopped by our new house to talk with Dad and check on how things were going. Dad explained the solution to the water problem they were working on. Mom asked about the bathroom, and Dad replied there was no sewage system to tie into. An outhouse would have to be constructed until the city installed a sewer line.

Mom was horrified and fed up with the city's lies about the sewage and water installation. We had listened to their conversations about this a number of times, only for Dad to walk away utterly frustrated. I'm not sure what transpired after this particular encounter, but when she reached home and walked in, she slammed the door behind her. We had been sitting on the floor watching TV, but that door slam quickly got our attention. She walked straight to the TV and turned it off.

"I need to talk with you all," she said, "but I will be back in a minute." She walked into the kitchen trying to get control of her emotions while we all sat quietly just looking at each other. She returned and began speaking.

"We will need to continue to heat water to take baths in the tubs we currently use." Her emotions were so palpable, we dared not ask a single question. "We will be making big changes, because we will not have a usable toilet or bathroom inside the house.

There is no sewage to run pipes, so your father will have to dig and build an outhouse for us."

What's an outhouse? I wondered.

"We will have to use a portable urine pot at night," she continued, "and they'll need to be carried out the following morning and emptied in the outhouse." After mom finished talking to us, she left the room.

I was sitting next to Abe, so I leaned over and whispered, "What's an outhouse?" He explained in detail for me to understand, and I was horrified. An outhouse within the City of Athens only four blocks from UGA? How degrading! Everyone else in the White communities had water and sewage.

Disappointments and deceptions were becoming insurmountable for my family. Issuing a permit to build a house in a designated urban renewal area, city officials' double-speak about the water and sewage, and now moving from a rental house to a new house with an outhouse—all of this was causing a great deal of friction between my mom and dad. This was very noticeable to us children, and their frustrations wore off on us. This was the first time I got to see how the city officials' misdeeds had been done time and time again to us. *It's so unjust!* I thought over and over.

Still, when our house was completed, we all walked in together and felt excited about moving in despite the embarrassing prospect of an outhouse. It was completed in late 1958, and our new address was 141 Peabody Street. There were about ten steps to walk up before reaching the front porch. The front door opened to the living room with a big oil heater—no more making fires in a fireplace and staying in bed waiting until the house warmed. The dining room and kitchen were to the right of the front door, and the kitchen had a pretty blue linoleum floor with a white flower pattern. The flooring in the other rooms was pine. The white kitchen sink was enclosed with a cabinet underneath. There was another long white wooden cabinet with shelves on the opposite wall. We had a white refrigerator and a white gas stove that was fueled by propane gas.

Mom said that the only furniture we needed was a table and enough chairs to put in the dining room so we could eat together. Enough seating for all of us was a nice change. The house had drywall and was painted throughout. There were three bedrooms: my mom and dad had one, my sisters and I shared one, and my brothers shared one. The bedrooms had nice double windows with closets for our clothes. It was a delightful difference to have a great deal of space in a new house, and we needed the extra space since we were growing up.

I give huge credit to the men of the community. They were highly skilled, capable, and worked as a team to build our house. They accomplished this despite the obstacles and disappointing setbacks.

We had grass in the front and back yards. A small tree in the backyard was out of the way of everyone, so we never played with it. At first it was very small, but then it started to grow. Mom noticed it was fruit-bearing and instructed us to leave this small tree alone. As weeks passed, the fruit started turning red, but it didn't resemble anything we had ever seen in the grocery store. Once the fruit was the size of a medium apple, Mom told us it was a pomegranate tree.

"A what?" we all asked in unison.

She picked one and opened it, then handed it to us. We reluctantly pulled the seeds out to try one or two but found it much too sour for our taste. Even without water or attention, this tree produced fruit each year, but we never pulled a single pomegranate from that day forward, and never tried eating it again.

Then came our next obstacle: Our school district was suddenly re-zoned. I was attending East Athens Elementary at the time, and we had all assembled at the bus pick-up area on the first day of school. We waited and waited, but the bus never came that morning. Upset parents, and other adults who were home, had to make arrangements for getting us to school and back home. They phoned the school district bus transportation department and all got the same reply: "We'll look into the matter." After several more calls, our parents were told that due to re-zoning of schools, there was a mix-up, and buses hadn't received information about our community. Our parents were upset with the school system for putting them in this predicament—none of the adults knew how the children were going to get to school.

Luckily, Dad came up with a solution. He purchased what looked like a black enclosed truck with a door that opened from the back. We children named it "Black Mariah." Dad removed all the seats from the back of this truck and placed large buckets upside down on each side of the truck's frame. All the neighborhood children met at the bottom of Lyndon Row and Cloverhurst for pick-up at the same time each morning. My dad would drive up, hop out, open the back door of the truck, and in we'd climb. We girls sat on the buckets or on older girls' laps. Boys sat on the floor of the truck. This was our transportation to and from school for weeks.

I understood from listening to our parents' conversations that some adults had been reaching out to the school transportation department for weeks. Our parents told us with uncertainty that we'd soon be getting bus pick-up for school. Neighbors in Linnentown encouraged my dad to apply for the job since he had been transporting us to and from school for months without incident. He did apply and waited to be contacted. Dad inquired about the position after not hearing back from the school district, and their feedback was brief: "You are not qualified."

Dad told us and everyone in the community what the school district had said. All the adults were in disbelief and furious about him not being offered the job. Preventing my father from pursuing a better job opportunity was another way of demonstrating who was in charge.

A few weeks later, the bus did come to pick us up. It was bus #34, and Doll White was the driver. The bus ride to our school was very long, and we had to adjust to all the bus stops and the long route. I remember the bus stopping in the White Hall community, which took thirty minutes to reach. From there, it was another thirty-plus minutes to school. The entire bus trip was too long and tiring. Sometimes we fell asleep and had to be awakened when the bus reached Linnentown.

Not only were we dealing with the transportation issue, but the rental housing on S. Finley had been torn down already and cleared prior to the spring of 1960. From that point until the spring of 1961, a large sign stood on Finley beside Creswell Hall dormitory as it was being constructed. The giant sign read: "University of Georgia Urban Renewal Area, Project No. GA R-50." This sign validated deep suspicions that had spread throughout our community. UGA wanted the property for expansion because it was only four blocks from their football stadium. Whatever was being built there was disrupting the entire community. Trucks and heavy equipment blocked driveways and street entrances. In front of homeowners' houses across the street from the former Doolittle property on Finley, tractors dug trenches the length of the street for big pipes and large cables. These deep trenches were not closed or covered during the day or night, so they were dangerous for us children. I remember getting off the school bus to walk to Aunt Bessie's house and having to jump over the open ditch before reaching her steps. Ditches being dug on both sides of the street was a wake-up call for all the adults.

Clearly, UGA had a plan that affected the entire community—it was being done in plain sight, and it was all legal. My emotions would stir every time I walked past that huge sign. I had never thrown a rock before, but I wanted to throw a rock at that sign. This act would have released some of stored anger and resentment that had escalated in me over the years. The adults read my mind, and other children's minds, too.

"Don't throw rocks at that sign," they warned us. We all replied in unison, "Yes, sir." But that didn't stop me from rolling my eyes at it.

The frustrations with the city and UGA were mounting. Athens had already approved an ordinance to pave Lyndon Row in its entirety and install street lights in January 1955, but nothing was done. In February 1959, an additional ordinance was approved to pave Peabody, South Finley, and Church in their entirety. Only Peabody was ever even partially paved. However, they never implemented any of the plans; instead, they helped UGA build dormitories on our land.

The adults had so many questions. How can an ordinance be approved and then just ignored? Why this blatant disrespect for an order? Was it to ensure this street was never paved to improve water and sewage infrastructure? It appeared that the city was not planning to spend our tax dollars to improve our community. Why was this ordinance approved on paper? Was it because the city knew about UGA's future project? Now the posting of the project sign was beginning to make sense: UGA wanted all the land in our community. Enlightenment brought unrest and the slowing or halting of some home improvement projects. Any and all monies had to be put aside for moving or relocating to a different neighborhood or to another city. Everything was changing quickly for us, but no one ever asked how we felt about it.

By 1960, my parents were openly discussing UGA wanting to take our community and our property. UGA wanted to expand, and Linnentown was in a prime location due to its close proximity to campus. Whenever I listened to them talking about it, I visualized a herd of elephants trampling toward our community; when they reached it, it would be destroyed, and there was no one in this entire city to steer them away from us.

This high-energy discussion among adults in the community always ended with total frustration. The adults were not getting many answers, and they remembered what had happened to the rental houses on South Finley Street just a few years prior, when that part of our neighborhood was sold by Mrs. Doolittle.

All home improvements in the community stopped because to the possibility of having to move at some point. My parents did the same. All the money they'd accumulated over the years to purchase our property on Peabody, the strategy they put in place to build our house by hiring skilled workmen from the community with minimal dollars, was only accomplished through community support and friendships. Knowing these accomplishments could not be repeated caused great frustration and anger. We felt trampled on, and were very hurt by the city's callous behavior and unjust treatment when we learned that UGA began an urban renewal project for their campus expansion—which included building dormitories for student housing in what was our neighborhood.

Regardless of the positive changes on campus, the feeling of apprehension was on the rise in our community, primarily due to the unknown. Not a single representative from the city of Athens or the University of Georgia came to inform our community. There was no communication of any kind to the homeowners—not a single letter, meeting, or phone call. The only notice we had were the words written on that big "urban renewal" sign in front of Creswell Hall. It indicated to us that UGA and the city of Athens were in partnership to make decisions about our future. Did anyone involved have a single concern about the horrendous impact this project would have on families? It was brutally apparent that no one cared about what would happen to us.

Concerns were heightening again in the summer of 1961, when White individuals started knocking on doors, explaining that each household in the community needed to fill out a "family survey form." One evening when I arrived home, I saw someone seated near Mom, asking question after question and writing on a form. Mom had a perplexed look as she attempted to answer each question about our house and family:

How many rooms are in the house?

How many adults and children live here?

What are the ages and genders of your children?

What is your household income?

Where are you thinking of relocating?

To that last question, my mother quietly replied, "East of Athens or outside the city limits."

My sisters and brothers and I always referred to an elephant when we were in troublesome situations. An elephant had not only entered the community but was now inside our house, holding us hostage. I felt as if that elephant were sucking all the oxygen from inside the room, for it was getting harder and harder to breathe as the questioning continued for what seemed like hours. We children were observing and being ever so still while we anxiously watched Mom's facial expressions.

When will the questions end? we all wondered.

Once the questionnaire was completed, Mom had a question of her own.

"What's the purpose of this survey and who's in charge of this project?" she asked.

The surveyor shrugged. "I'm just completing the survey and will turn it in. Don't know who's in charge."

With that, the elephant slowly turned and left. We were all quiet for a while.

"Well damn," Mom finally said. "I answered all those questions and did not get a single answer for the two questions I asked."

She told us the paperwork had something we do with us having to move, but she didn't know how it was connected.

"We would like to know what the hell is going on, so we can prepare to move!" she exclaimed. "Why can't one person come here to communicate what is going on?"

A feeling of total hopelessness came over me, something I had never felt before. How can your own city allow one of its communities to be treated this way? Was it because this community was poor? Or because we were Black? Or both? Was anyone considering the families?

Families who moved to the neighborhood stayed for decades, even generations; there wasn't much transition. Most adults had aged in place and had hearing, visual, and mental impairments. Neighbors grew more and more concern about them and did their best to explain why they had to move, even though they owned their homes. The hardest hit were the elderly without family, and it was painful not being able to help with getting housing. Some of the elderly who were on social security—especially widows—could not afford home maintenance, so their homes were in disrepair. And yet ... these White surveyors were knocking on the doors of our neighborhood, blithely asking questions in order to complete their "Family Survey Form."

Neighbors knew that some people could not possibly answer the questions, and it's likely that some couldn't complete the forms at all. If the community had been informed and involved, the survey form could have been completed by a person of their choosing, instead of individuals they were uncomfortable with and did not trust. When some families began to move, my family and a few others were uncertain how we should plan to move, without having an understanding of how much money we would receive after final calculations were complete. We had filled out the family survey form but had received no information on who to contact for questions or timeline of property acquisition.

"When will checks need to be picked up?" I heard my dad say to my mom in frustration. "How soon will we have to move out, once the check is received? Do these people think we all have money? We certainly can't get into another house until we are paid!"

My mother just shook her head and sighed. Most of us did not have money in any bank—we had to borrow from a finance company, friend, family, or employer. Moving away from this community was unsettling. The fears of my parents and our neighbors had transferred to me and my siblings. Where were we moving to?

This was the only community we had known. We were comfortable there and had a great deal of support from all our neighbors.

I knew I had to adjust, for we had to move.

Elephants had been set in motion, and there was no help coming to steer them away from Linnentown.

With many of my neighbors feeling exhausted and out of options, they began moving away from Linnentown one by one. I remember Mr. John and Mrs. Julia Griffin moving, and I learned that Mr. John was notified of the acquisition of his property with just a torn piece of notebook paper. Also attached was a notification of the rent amount and start date if it was still occupied the month rent was due. After Mr. John contacted the city of Athens, he was given a time and date to come and sign paperwork and pick up his check. He received a check for $2,010 for his property—an insulting and degrading amount. This was not enough for them to buy another house. They ended up moving to a small house in the backyard of a large White family, where Mr. John would work as a gardener and Mrs. Julia as a maid.

This was not good news for us. Instead of our neighbors moving forward with this relocation, I saw them moving backward. It looked like sharecropping all over again. This was an unspoken thought that I and others shared with a shaking of our heads after hearing about the move. How could this happen? It was all very unsettling to me. A few weeks after they had moved, I was saddened to see their empty house. I missed seeing their smiling faces and hearing Mrs. Julia say hello as we passed by.

Then there was Freddie Mae's family. They lived in a very nice wood frame house on 183 Lyndon Row. Their house would've equaled any other middle-class neighborhood in the city. Her uncle, Mr. Chill, had added two rooms extending from the back; one was a room and the other a bathroom. Her mother, Mrs. Susie Mae, decided that only colorful plumbing fixtures, bathtub, sink, and commode would be installed. When she and her husband saved enough money, the house was electrically wired for wall switches instead of strings to operate ceiling lights.

Mrs. Susie Mae also selected and decorated their house with nice furniture. Freddie's parents were a hardworking team who saved money to accomplish all purchases and home improvements. This is why they owned two houses in the neighborhood. Her two uncles lived in their other house further down the street. Freddie's family was financially able to relocate to a newly constructed home on the east side of town. But they were the exception; most families were not so fortunate. When their urban renewal acquisition paperwork was ready to be filled out, Freddie's parents contacted her to come home from college to assist with the paperwork. She had already graduated from high school and was attending Spelman College in Atlanta when we moved from Linnentown.

After signing all the paperwork, they received a check for only $4,750. They used this to buy a new home and a car, but the city charged them $45 a month for rent until they relocated. This was another tactic to get families to move quickly. Once the city acquired a property, that property owner became a tenant of the city and had to pay rent until relocation. Rents ranged from $15.00 to $86.25 per month. Families focused on putting money aside to move and pay rent on short notice. Purchasing a car came with more monthly expenses: gas, car maintenance, and insurance. Freddie's family did not own a car, as her parents were in walking distance of their jobs at UGA.

Freddie had several relatives in the community. An aunt lived next door, two uncles lived together further down Lyndon Row, another uncle lived on Lyndon Row at a different address, and a great-uncle lived on Finley Street. Freddie Mae was a few years older than my older sister and brother.

Bobby Crook's family, Mr. Roy and Essie Crook at 167 Peabody, lived in a large house at the top of the hill and owned another lot behind their house. Mr. Roy Cook was employed at a fraternity house on the UGA campus. Their home was also used as a bed and breakfast and was one of the main places Black people stayed when visiting our town before integration. Their house was solidly built and beautifully maintained, and they had a chicken coop in their backyard. Standing in their living room, Bobby and his father could see the 50-yard line of UGA's Sanford Stadium— sharing this story always brought a smile to Bobby's face. His family was the last to move out in 1966. Not only were they looking for a house, they were also looking for one big enough to continue their bed-and-breakfast business. His parents were assessed a ten-dollar monthly rent until they were able to relocate.

Mr. Roy was interested in purchasing a lot on Church Street near their house on Peabody, but the city refused to sell this lot to them because it was not zoned for building a house. They purchased a house on Plaza Street and moved there in 1966. Bobby had a particularly bad experience that has stayed in his memory ever since moving from the community. His dog, Lady, had been missing late one evening, and did not come back by nightfall. However, Bobby assured himself Lady would return sometime overnight. The following morning, Bobby awoke to silence—no dog was barking. He immediately got up, dressed, and started looking outside for her. He found Lady at the bottom of an open trench that the city dug on his street, and thankfully he was able to get her out. Luckily, she was not hurt and he was greatly relieved. But this should not have happened.

Two houses up from us lived another friendly elderly neighbor, Mrs. Nellie Johnson. Shortly after Mr. John and Mrs. Julia moved, Mrs. Nellie and her daughter and grandson, who lived with her, did too. They purchased a house on Benning Street near Baxter, a short street with only about eight houses. The top of the street had a steep grade that flattened toward the bottom. Their house was the last one on the street and had a small creek that ran beside their house and past the dead-end post. One summer during a rain downpour, the water from the creek started to overflow and water reach their front yard. Her daughter came out of their house and realized the water was still rising. They managed to move the car, but the water steadily rose up over their steps to the front porch.

The Johnsons were horrified to realize they had purchased a house in a flood zone. Each time it rained heavily the creek overflowed, and when the water receded, it left a huge mess. They asked their city councilman for help over and over, but it fell on deaf ears. The neighbors started calling our local newspaper, the *Athens Banner Herald*, and they printed pictures of the flood in the paper. That got someone's attention and the city finally did something, but it didn't erase the fact that the Johnsons had just moved from an urban renewal area to another horrendous housing area.

In Linnentown, I watched bulldozers demolish empty houses. Each time I saw a house razed to the ground, I felt as if a family had been discarded after giving years of support to the community. It was heartbreaking to see my community torn down day by day. Some families let people know where they were moving, but some just left without saying a word. This was understandable, as some of them were moving to not necessarily good places.

Only three houses from Linnentown were physically moved

to different parts of Athens. Davis Johnson relocated a house from Peabody to East Broad Street and a family is currently (in 2021) living in this house. Ben and Louise Taylor moved their house from Lyndon Row to Glenhaven Avenue, where a family member is still also living. Roy and Nancy Williams moved their house from Peabody to the West Hancock extension. Nancy, the original homeowner, is still living in her house. At 101 years old, she can still recall the nasty comments directed at Black homeowners.

"I hope to live to see justice done," she said recently.

One night, I found my mother at the dining room table crying—something I had never seen before. She was having a panic attack, and she gasped for air as tears rolled down her cheeks. My heart grieved for her and I broke down myself. In between sobs, she said she was just overwhelmed with us having to move, not knowing where we were moving or how we would get there. There was nothing I or anyone else in the room could do to console her.

"Where are we moving to?" she said through her tears. "Where are we going to live?"

After a long while that seemed like forever to me, she was able to calm herself.

With all the planning that had taken place between UGA and the city, had anyone given a thought about how the urban renewal would affect families? This is a question I still ask myself, and the likely answer saddens me. The elephants were on their way and they were in full throttle to reach our community. This was one sleepless night for me and very unsettling for a long time.

A number of our neighbors had been notified of the date of their property acquisition. There was a designated room at City Hall where we were to sign paperwork and receive checks for properties. But there were no negotiations for the properties. In some instances, as soon as the City bought a house in Linnentown—for pennies on the dollar—it was razed by bulldozers, a repeat of what had occurred on Finley Street. Because of this demolition, there was only one way to enter and exit the community. Starting at the entrance of the community, heavy equipment started digging deep horizontal ditches in front of houses, no matter if they were empty or occupied, and large pipes were put in.

Once the ditches were wide open, they remained left open as workers continued down the street to a designated point. No cover, tape, or sign was posted to alert the community of these open ditches, so getting off the school bus and walking home was dangerous—we were forced to jump over open holes or ditches to get home. The workers showed no compassion for our community. Streets in the neighborhood were closed off, and heavy equipment would run at midnight right up against homes. There were many sleepless nights. All of this reinforced the feeling of being kicked out.

I could not understand why some of the most solid and beautifully built homes in our community were receiving such miserably low amounts of money, particularly when they were comparable to houses in White middle-class neighborhoods. To add insult to injury, some Blacks outside Linnentown had been labeled "community leaders" by White city officials in Athens. These individuals were called upon when Athens needed token "diverse representation" to speak for people in the community or to get their input. The people in Linnentown did not know if these so-called leaders had been involved in the urban renewal project, for they did not live in or come to Linnentown to talk with homeowners.

I call these "yes people," for they were sought after to supposedly represent segments of the people whenever there was a need for "diversity." But leadership representation should belong to residents who are affected, not those who would suffer no consequences. If only someone had come to our community and just listened to the homeowners.

Chapter Four
MOVING TIME

One Saturday morning while we were eating breakfast, Abe and Katie told the rest of the siblings that we would be moving soon. We immediately stopped mid-bite and clamored in unison.

"Where??" we asked.

"Public housing," Abe responded. "Rocksprings Homes."

We all knew where Rocksprings Homes was located. Katie told us there wasn't enough money to rent a house or an apartment or even to cover all the utilities. Our application had been approved, so we were waiting to be contacted about a move-in date. We didn't ask any additional questions. We finished breakfast, then left to play outside.

Mom did not speak about the move; she just hid her

uneasiness by spending more time in the kitchen, cooking. One evening, I decided to join her, as I did periodically to observe, so I could learn to cook. While I was assisting, she gave directions on how to mix or add to the pan of what was cooking.

"I've been giving cooking instructions at work today and most of this week," she told me.

Her comment surprised me, as Mom rarely talked about work.

"Cooking instructions to who?" I asked. "Another cook?"

She shook her head and looked at me with a smile on her face. I had not seen her smile for a while, so I was instantly delighted. It was a special moment between mother and daughter. She answered my question while I listened intently.

"Well," she said, stirring some soup, "you know we just hired Sally, our new cook." I nodded. Sally had replaced the previous cook, who had quit.

"Sally is extremely helpful with keeping all dishes, pots, and pans washed, dried, and put away, and she keeps the steam table clean," Mom said. The steam table required constant attention due to food spills. "But at work today, the other cooks and I discovered that Sally can't cook!"

"What?!" I exclaimed, eager for details. It was uncommon for me to be privy to a little gossip. My smile continued to broaden with each detail my mom recounted.

They were in a predicament as to what to do, as everyone in the kitchen knew Sally needed her job, but they needed her to cook, not clean. They did not want to tell their supervisor, because Sally would have been fired. They talked amongst themselves, and after a short discussion, they agreed the work Sally was doing each day was most helpful because it allowed them to focus on just cooking, which appeared to be working somewhat better than having everyone cooking. They all agreed to let Sally continue cleaning, but they added some chores to her responsibilities. The other cooks asked Mom to convey their decision to Sally, who was delighted with the arrangement. She was happy to keep her job, and the other cooks were happy to not wash dishes!

The new responsibilities among the team were never communicated to their supervisor. I was amazed the person in charge of hiring did not know Sally couldn't cook. Did they just assume she could, or did Sally tell them she could, when in fact she could not? Was it because she needed a job? Mom just smiled and said, "It worked out for all involved." Our smiles turned to laughter when she finished telling me this story. I have always counted those few minutes spent in the kitchen with my mom as very special, and this story has stayed with me ever since.

Many years later, in 1974, I was hired as an entry-level employee at a manufacturing plant in Athens. I was promoted to supervisor two years later, and later I moved up to operations leader. My entire responsibility pertained to operations in personnel, safety, quality, and productivity. There were many times when I relied on my mom's experience when I encountered challenging situations at work. Her story about a team of cooks willing to help a new employee helped guide my approach to problem-solving.

Allowing my own teams to work together on a variety of issues such as productivity and quality resulted in better performance because they were all involved in the decision-making. This approach often produced improved procedures, productivity output, teamwork, and morale. It created team "buy-in" and often resulted in an improved, profitable operation for the area and company. While my successful twenty-seven years in management was due to a great deal of extensive training, the common-sense approach to problem-solving that my mom taught me helped me the most.

One evening back in Linnentown while Dad and Mom were away, my brother Abe told me that the property acquisition had been completed. Our parents never discussed with us what had occurred. My mom always needed to help Dad with any type of paperwork since he could not read. Abe said the check for our property was $4,750. I'm sure my parents would have received more money if they had been able to afford an attorney to advocate for them—other homeowners who had used attorneys had received a bigger check than those who had no one to represent them. But Mom was done fighting or discussing; she just wanted to move on.

Shortly afterward, Mom was contacted by public housing to pay deposits and was given a date when an apartment would be available for us to move. We only had a short time to pack and move.

Through no fault of their own, some families were making the degrading transition from being homeowners to living in public housing—from building real wealth to losing it all at once. My family was one of those. It was a tough pill to swallow, but we really didn't have a choice. We surely didn't have the power to fight back.

Despite our sadness, we had to leave Linnentown and establish a new place to live in Rocksprings Homes. We moved on a Saturday morning in the fall of 1962. By the following Sunday, we had everything unpacked and set up at 165 Rocksprings Homes. I had classmates who lived there, but it was strange being in such close proximity to neighbors. During the first winter there, we all had trouble sleeping at night. It was too hot inside the apartment at night, and we all caught terrible colds. Mom decided to cut off the one gas heater at night. From then on, we slept better and our colds cleared up.

I started ninth grade soon after we moved to Rocksprings. I felt awkward about my height and nervous about adapting to high school. My only comfort about this transition was that Katie and Abe were there. They were both seniors. Abe was not willing to attend first grade without Katie, so Mom enrolled them together, even though Katie was a year younger. They were in the first grade at Union Baptist Institute in Linnentown—which closed shortly after they started school, as it was part of the urban renewal project. By the time Katie and Abe graduated in 1963, the school's name was still Athens High and Industrial, but in 1964 it changed to Burney-Harris High School. It was the only Black high school in Athens at the time.

Miss Elizabeth E. King, the girls' basketball coach, had spotted me in the hallway one day, which was not hard to do since I was a head taller than most of my classmates. I was walking to my next class when she briefly stopped me by her classroom's doorway. Touching my arm, she said, "You look like a basketball player. You have the height and size. Are you trying out for the basketball team this year?"

"Yes, ma'am," I said.

"Have you ever played basketball before?" she asked.

I shifted my books and admitted that I hadn't.

"But I'm looking forward to learning how to play," I said eagerly. "I've learned some basics playing in pickup games. And I've been practicing shooting hoops in P.E. on school days."

She smiled and said, "I'm looking forward to working with you on the court."

I floated down the hallway. This short interaction energized me to work harder in P.E. before basketball tryouts. I had to remind myself that football cheerleader tryouts were on my list as well.

Basketball tryouts were physically hard and mentally tough. After my first few practices, I couldn't raise my right arm the next morning without feeling excruciating pain. Mom put a heating pad on my arm for a few evenings, and the soreness faded after the first week. During each practice, Miss King kept a keen eye on all players on the court, while giving helpful tips to improve our moves, whether shooting or guarding. Her assistant, Eugene "Doc" Holmes, was always there to give assistance as needed.

Initially, girls only played half court, then evolved to a full-court game. We all practiced hard, since we knew Miss King would make the roster in the next few weeks. When she blew the last whistle one evening, signaling the end of practice, she had us come sit on the benches in front of her. She said she'd seen a lot of talent on the practice floor and appreciated everybody trying out, but she could only add a limited number of players to the current team.

Doc Holmes started calling names from a prepared list. I waited anxiously, and then I heard my name. I had made the cut!

Playing basketball for my high school made me feel optimistic and raised my self-esteem. I accomplished one of the two personal goals set before entering high school: I wanted to be part of team sports and I wanted to represent my school. Happily, basketball was affordable—I only had to purchase a pair of high-top sneakers. The school provided the uniform, and there was no registration fee. Even though I didn't get any basketball playing time as a ninth grader, I learned a great deal about ball handling and shooting techniques. Most importantly, I learned how to be part of a team.

I also enjoyed cheerleading and traveling with the football team for away games. The highlight of away games in Atlanta was eating fried chicken at Paschal's Restaurant. Their soul food was delicious. The school provided our cheering unforms, and again there was no registration fee. My grades in my core classes improved, I was studying more at home, I had new friends, and I was making a good impression on my teachers. I was finally in a state of peace and started smiling more.

But then the unthinkable happened.

One night, my sisters and brothers and I overheard our parents arguing, something about our move from Linnentown. Their tone was unsettling. Listening from the girls' bedroom, we asked each other when and why had they started talking to each other this way. And why were they arguing about Linnentown? We knew our dad wasn't happy with the move, but we had been at Rocksprings Homes for months already. Clearly, it was still an issue. Dad had not wanted to move into public housing—he had been raised on a farm, and after my parents got married they moved to Linnentown, next door to my great-grandmother. He had wanted to move his family to a house in the country, but he didn't have the money or the support to make it happen.

At some point, I started blocking out all conversations between my parents, unless one of them called my name and I had to respond. The edginess of their voices affected me greatly and I had a hard time sleeping at night. The next week, my father told us that he and my mom were separating. My siblings and I were heartbroken. He said he would be back for us when he was able to rent a house, and then he left. My mom moved out as well and promised she would be back when she was able to save enough money to rent a house.

Four of us kids stayed in the apartment: Abe, Katie, Pepper, and me. Abe and Katie had already graduated from high school and were working every day. My sister Pete stayed with Aunt

Bessie and Uncle Dave, both retired by then. They had purchased a house a few blocks down from Rocksprings Homes. My younger sister and brother, Marion and Alex, would stay with Aunt Lila Mae and Uncle Joe until my father came back for us. They lived in Rocksprings Homes and had ten children of their own, but they made room for two more.

As a result of having been abruptly booted out of Linnentown, our family was now split up into five fragments. I'm pretty sure my parents would have stayed together if UGA and the city had just let us be. We all would have flourished in Linnentown. But now I found myself adjusting yet again, this time without parents, Marion, or Alex. And to make things worse, we had no car and no public transportation.

Katie, Pepper, and I were awakened by Abe early one Saturday morning.

"Be back in a while," he said, shutting the front door behind him. We mumbled "OK" and went back to sleep.

A few hours later, we were awakened again by a car horn honking noisily nonstop. We got up and looked out the window—and there was Abe, sitting in the driver's seat of a blue and white two-door Dodge.

With a wide smile on his face, he motioned for us to come outside. We threw on some clothes and were out the door in a flash. The car was old, but it was his. Katie and Pepper and I thought it looked really sharp. Some of the paint was missing but it was clean—and most importantly, we now had transportation! This brought smiles to our faces and joy to our hearts, which we all greatly needed. Later that day, Abe surprised me with something else.

"I'm gonna take you to get your driver's license on your birthday," he said with a grin. I reacted to that with eyes as big as tennis balls, a huge hug, and an ear-to-ear smile. Even though my birthday wasn't until the next year, just the thought made me giddy.

This was the summer of 1963. I'd just completed my ninth-grade year with a B+ grade point average and felt good about that. There wasn't much for a fifteen-year-old girl to do in these apartments, so I mostly listened to music and watched TV. I wanted to improve my basketball skills, but there was no place to practice within walking distance. As a result, I had to wait for school to start and practice in the gym.

We stayed pretty close to home that summer, but would frequently check in on Marion and Alex at Aunt Lila Mae's house. Mom and Dad regularly came by to see us and left money with Abe or Katie for our care. I started working as a part-time waitress whenever there was a banquet at the Continuing Education building at UGA, and working there gave me the money to buy clothes and shoes for the upcoming school year. Looking back, I realize that I was living according to the standards my parents had taught us and the same standards that I still value today: self-motivation, a strong work ethic, and setting goals.

I was sitting on the front porch at home one summer evening when a friend walked up and asked me to come with her to buy a soda at a nearby apartment. When we arrived, I saw that the family who lived there were also selling hotdogs, potato chips, and Kool-Aid. They were trying to raise money to help another family in the complex whose daughter would be attending college that fall.

I bought a soda and dropped nickels into a large 64-oz. tin can on top of the kitchen table. The tin can was a familiar sight—in Linnentown, this size of tin can was used to collect money at a community fish fry for a poor family in our neighborhood. Other residents bought food and drinks at the apartment, and the lady who waited on us thanked us for helping their neighbor's daughter go to college. I left feeling good about how our community was stepping up to support a family that was not able to pay for their child to attend college. This fundraiser would have a lasting impact on me.

I began tenth grade in the fall of 1963. At the same time, Abe announced he was getting married and moving out. I should have been happy for him, but I was so disappointed—it was just another blow to our already tenuous situation. I loved my brother and only wanted the best for him, but it was hard to deal with yet another big change. During the days leading up to Abe's move, I felt empty and was unable to talk to him about his leaving. I finally had to adjust my selfish feelings and embrace his new-found happiness. On the day he was moving, I hugged him tightly as he carried his last package to his car. I cried after he left, for I knew that I would miss his presence and support. He said he would come by to check on us periodically, and he was just a phone call away if we needed him. I was quite downcast. Just as I had adjusted in the past, I needed to do it again.

As I continued playing basketball, my skill level improved to the point that our coach put me in at a big game. Practices at school each weekday, followed by a two-mile walk home, kept me away from home and was an excuse for not completing my homework. I also continued cheerleading. My core class grades slipped to about a "C" average, which did not concern me. No one was asking me about school or grades. As a result, I developed somewhat of a lazy attitude, and that affected my self-esteem. I missed my parents and needed their discipline.

The only thing exciting about the summer of 1964 was my sixteenth birthday in July. Abe was true to his word: He took me to the State Patrol's office to take the driver's exam. I passed the test and walked away with my driver's license! It was the highlight of my summer. Abe allowed me to drive him to work most days so I could keep his car to visit friends and have fun. I would drive a lot of miles by the time I picked him up from work, so the gas tank was almost always on empty. Nevertheless, Abe forgave me and would fill it up himself. He was a very generous and loving older brother.

Periodically, I bumped into someone from Linnentown, usually at the grocery store, as the property acquisitions were still being made until 1966. It was always a delight to see and talk with anyone from our old neighborhood. I was anxious to hear any news about my old community: who still lived there, who had recently moved out, and where they had moved to. One day, I was told houses were still being demolished, and all street entrances and exits had been closed except one. The next piece of information I received was devastating: The fire department had burned down our house. Although it had been a couple of years since we had moved, the news was still disturbing. I had held on to the hope that our house could be moved to a different part of the city, since the men in the community had built it. I craved any information about what was happening to the land our community had been built on and often reminisced about my old friends and their families.

I started eleventh grade year in the fall of 1964. I stood 5'10" in my bare feet and was the tallest girl in my class—even taller than most boys. My new growth and improved ball handling and shooting gave me an advantage on the basketball court. Miss King told me I'd be on the starting lineup. I began to average double-digit points most games, which delighted me, and winning a game always put me in a state of perfect bliss.

I also continued cheerleading for football. Even though I wasn't really excited about cheering, it was still better than going home to an empty apartment. Some friends were already making decisions about college and their future careers. I couldn't allow myself to think about that. I was not prepared, and besides, I didn't have the money. However, I did think about going into manufacturing. I managed to maintain a "C" average for the school year and was promoted to the twelfth grade.

I had no plans for the summer of 1965, so I simply stayed close to home and worked as a waitress and also at the Georgia Center for Continuing Education at UGA. I didn't work many hours working there, but I saved whatever I earned, and it was enough to buy clothing and shoes. Abe had moved out, so I didn't have any access to a car anymore. My friend Sarah Guilliam's father had a few nice cars, though, and he allowed her to drive one periodically. She would come by and pick me up to ride around with her occasionally—a nice reprieve from the long boring summer days.

In the fall of 1965, I started my senior year. I decided to put all my energy into playing basketball and graduating the following May. True to his word, my dad moved back to the apartment with us before school started. About the same time, Katie announced she would be moving into an apartment on Glenhaven Avenue, within walking distance of our place. I knew I'd miss her, for she had always been there for me and had always given me solid advice when I asked for it, or when she thought I needed it. But since Dad was back home, Katie's leaving was not as disruptive and sad as it otherwise would have been. It was great to have him back; his presence brought comfort and order to our home. Plus, he brought happy news: He had found a home nearby and we would move there in a few months!

With my stabilizing home situation, I was finally able to focus on improving my basketball game by spending more time on the court and practicing after school. I deeply desired to increase my shooting average in my senior year, and Miss King encouraged me every step of the way. At the end of the season, I averaged double figures in points and rebounds and was named most valuable player! I also continued as a cheerleader my senior year, even though I had decided to quit when Dad moved home so I could spend time with him. Dad wanted me to keep cheering.

In the spring of 1966, with a few months to go before graduation, all my classmates were talking about their prom escorts. No one had asked me, and I did not have a dress, but I was still planning to go. My grandmother made me a short black dress, and it looked nice on me. Finally, my friend Reginald asked me to the prom, and I happily said yes. But the night before the dance, Reginald wrecked his parents' car, and he was grounded.

I was devastated. I had a beautiful dress and really wanted to go, but who would come with me on such short notice? After much thought, I asked my brother Abe to escort me, and he said he'd love to. I was so relieved!

That evening, Abe came over and patiently waited for me to get ready while he visited with family. When I walked into the room, he got up.

"Well don't you look lovely!" he exclaimed.

"Thank you, Abe," I said with a smile. "And you are looking handsome tonight!"

I slipped my arm in his and we walked out the door. He was the perfect gentleman that night, opening and closing doors and leading me up the steps to our school's gym, where the prom was being held. He escorted me inside and was walking me to a table when I overheard some girls in my class making sarcastic remarks.

"Her brother is her escort?!" whispered one girl with a sneer. "What, she couldn't get a date?"

Their rudeness didn't bother me. I was just happy Abe had changed his plans for me and I was delighted to be with him at the prom. We danced, had fun, and were in plenty of photos that night. To this day I still smile whenever I look at the picture of me with my older brother Abe at Spring Prom in 1966.

A few weeks later, I graduated from Burney-Harris High School. While getting ready in my cap and gown, I reflected on all the obstacles my family and I had overcome to get to this point. I definitely became a stronger person as a result of all I had experienced at my young age. After all, we had been evicted from our beloved and happy home in Linnentown, and then our parents had divorced almost immediately after our move to the apartment. But I had to count my blessings: My parents were always there to love and support us, and they had raised us with rock-solid standards—by which we lived even after both had moved out. The values they taught us were imprinted on our characters from a very young age, and not even divorce and family separation could change that.

I had also been pondering the course my life would take after graduation. Should I apply to a technical school for management courses, or apply for a job in manufacturing to get on-the-job experience? I didn't have transportation or money, so either choice would involve some hard work and sacrifice. For the first time in my young life, I had to make a decision about my direction entirely on my own.

My dad knew I was giving a lot of thought to my options and asked if we could talk. We sat at the kitchen table and he began revisiting at length what we had been through as a family in

Linnentown up to our present situation. Then he asked if I planned to move with him, Marion, and Alex to the new place he had found. Finding the words to talk with him was difficult, but I managed.

I told him I wanted to apply to a technical school to take management courses, but I didn't have money or transportation. If I couldn't make that work, I would apply for a manufacturing job and would carpool until I was able to purchase a used car. I planned to stay with Katie (she had earlier agreed) while I looked for a job. Dad supported my plans and told me that if anything changed, I was always welcome to live with him and my younger brother and sister. I was so grateful for his attitude. He encouraged and respected me as an adult, but he still loved me like his little girl and was there to take care of me if I needed it.

Along with a few other friends and recent graduates, I began completing job applications at manufacturing sites. I received a call one day, and a company representative asked if I could start work the following week. I accepted the offer and started immediately, happily reporting to my first job. I was looking forward to writing the next chapter in my life and was all smiles. Although I only planned to work with the company for one year, I stayed for twenty-seven years before retiring.

But I never anticipated what would happen decades later that would bring my life back full circle to where it all began: Linnentown.

Chapter Five

GIVING VOICE TO LINNENTOWN

One evening in September 2019, I received a call from Geneva Johnson Eberhart, one of the first descendants from Linnentown. She told me that a young man named Dr. Joseph Carter had phoned her, looking for descendants of Linnentown homeowners. Joseph was a community organizer and labor researcher in Athens, and he was investigating Linnentown's erasure due to an urban renewal project in the 1960s. Joseph had found the documented data leading up to the day the city of Athens and the University of Georgia took our property away. With this information in hand, he wanted to talk with anyone who once lived in Linnentown. In a daze, I told Geneva to give Joseph my name and phone number.

My mind was reeling. For so many years I had wanted more

information on why and how the city had done this to our families, and now someone—someone who cared about Linnentown—had found the answers. Long-suppressed emotions surfaced, and they were hard to contain. After Geneva and I ended our call, I just sat for a few minutes, holding my cell phone. *Finally*, I thought, *just maybe . . . just maybe what occurred decades ago will be brought to light.*

With that one thought, tears started flowing.

Joseph called me one evening the following week. He politely introduced himself and shared a little about his research and how he found the urban-renewal data that led to Linnentown's erasure. The next time we met was in the Athens-Clarke County Library, where he showed me data he had found archived in the Hargrett Rare Book and Manuscript Library at UGA. The name "Linnentown" appears nowhere in city or university records—as though it never existed—so I was shocked that Joseph knew about us.

He pulled a form out of a folder and handed it to me. I immediately recognized the same "Family Survey Form" I had witnessed my mother answering questions in our living room in 1961. A rush of sad memories turned into tears as I read it slowly. At the bottom of the first page, I read a handwritten note: "House completely collapsed—burned by Athens Fire Department."

I was hurt and angered simultaneously. How could our home, built by the men in the community, be burned to ashes? Our house was a symbol of what the community men had accomplished together—and the fire department had just torched it without a second thought. I realized I hadn't take a breath for a while and inhaled sharply. I exhaled slowly, shaking my head.

I finally got control of my emotions and started telling Joseph about life in our Black community. We talked until closing time and figured out a plan to get in touch with more descendants.

When we parted, I somehow felt stronger, empowered to right the wrongs that had occurred so many years ago to my parents, relatives, and Linnentown neighbors. I knew it wouldn't be easy, but it was work that needed to be done.

At home, I reread the survey form again, going over each of my mother's answers. I clearly remembered that evening when a stranger quizzed her for personal information that must have been uncomfortable to share. The form listed gross annual income for my family as $2,544, with a question mark for gross monthly. Dad was unemployed at the time. Mom listed her earnings as eighty dollars a month. Sixteen-year-old Abe's monthly income was fifty dollars, fifteen-year-old Katie's was thirty-seven dollars, and fourteen-year-old Pepper's income was fifty dollars month. They all worked during the summer months, but none had full-time jobs. Why was their income listed in the yearly calculations? They were teenagers!

When the survey was completed on August 12, 1961, my parents' mortgage balance was $1,200, and the monthly payments were fifty-one dollars. In less than two years, my parent would have owned the house. Instead, we were forced to move to public housing, and my parents never became homeowners again. What the city of Athens and UGA had done was unspeakably unjust and criminal.

The sadness and anger combined to create a fierce determination I had never experienced before, and it lit a fire within me. I was moved to write and speak publicly to raise awareness about Linnentown, which I had not previously done. I phoned my two sisters and shared with them the story of Joseph's retrieval of the archived documents and our plans to organize first descendants. Just as I had, both my sisters experienced a range of emotions as they were taken back down memory lane to Linnentown. And just like me, they were both fiercely determined to go to work.

I made phone calls to other first descendants whom I had only talked with in passing, mainly at grocery stores. More phone calls led to discussions about their involvement and a need for a strategy to raise awareness of what had happened to our neighborhood in the 1960s. The wider Athens community had never heard of Linnentown; only select groups involved, along with our families, employers, and friends, knew about it. There had been no newspaper coverage of the UGA project other than one small mention, and it said nothing about Linnentown. *The Red & Black*, a student newspaper, quoted the newly hired UGA Housing director as saying hard work would go into giving "the girls [in the newly constructed Brumby Hall] a sense of belonging."[1]

This part of our history had been lost to the public for decades, and only oral history accounts were being passed down through our families. We were ready to speak when called upon, or to engage with community members, politicians, and small groups. This is how everything changed for Linnentown.

September 12, 2019, was an incredible day. Our first organized forum was a special collaboration between Historic Athens and the Linnentown Project, with film support provided by organizations like Below Baldwin and Enlightened Media Productions. The Athens-Clarke County Mayor's Office gave a generous research grant, and we held a well-attended forum at the Lyndon House Arts Center. Geneva Johnson Eberhart, Christine Davis Johnson, and I spoke passionately about our lives in Linnentown. Commissioner Mariah Parker attended the meeting, and afterward Joseph approached her

---

[1] "Brumby Means Luxury," *The Red and Black*, September 22, 1966, https://gahistoricnewspapers.galileo.usg.edu/lccn/gua1179162/1966-09-22/ed-1/seq-25/#index=0&rows=12&proxtext="Brumby+Means+Luxury%22&sequence=0&words=Brumby+Luxury+Means&page=1.

and asked if she would be willing to champion a resolution and present it the Athens-Clarke County mayor and commission.

Her response brought us great hope and joy. This was exactly the reason she ran for office, she said: to champion those in the community who had been treated unjustly and to be a vehicle of change by being a voice for the voiceless. She was excited to help. We were delighted to have her on board, for we knew she would engage other commissioners to enlighten them and try to get their support.

The first descendants meeting was held at my house on a beautiful Sunday evening on October 19, 2019. What a reunion! Some of us had not seen each other in decades. We talked and shared stories until Joseph brought our meeting to order. He led a focused strategy meeting on how to raise awareness in the entire city, as well as the whole state of Georgia. We organized ourselves as "The Linnentown Project" and agreed that our mission would be to educate the citizens of Athens and to seek justice for the harms that had been done to Linnentown. This would require a great deal of work, but we were up to the challenge.

We agreed on strategies for contacting and informing key individuals, then asking for their support. We developed four key goals of the project:

(1) Develop a clear purpose: To educate others about the harmful effects of urban renewal on Black communities and to advocate for reparations through the Linnentown Resolution,

(2) Complete all data collection and analysis before any community organizing,

(3) Develop the reparational audit, and

(4) Establish a working team to execute the project's purpose.

Joseph explained that the next order of business would be to write a resolution—a form of local legislation that documented oral and written history of Linnentown's beginning, as far back as possible. It would include details about the people of Linnentown, including the adults' job skills, and every particular of what had occurred during the urban renewal project, starting with the arrival of the heavy equipment in 1958 and ending when the last family moved out in 1966. This document, Joseph explained, would also include "resolves"—our petitions for reparations—and would have a summary of pertinent archived data.

After several days of collaborative writing, we had a full first draft. We named it "The Linnentown Resolution for Recognition and Redress." It was a proud moment for us, and we planned how to lobby the Athens-Clarke County mayor and commission to adopt it.

Before writing the resolution, we discussed the importance of the precise language to accurately describe what had happened to us. We agreed that "White supremacy" was the exact phrase to use when describing the urban renewal partnership between the city of Athens and UGA, and that "terrorism" was also the correct word for describing how UGA treated our families in order to quickly move us out.

We agreed on eight specific, concrete petitions in the resolution:

(1) Acknowledge the injustices committed against Linnentown,

(2) Erect an on-site Wall of Recognition as a permanent acknowledgement of our once-thriving community,

(3) Empower the Linnentown descendants to make annual county budget recommendations as a form of equitable redress,

(4) Erect historical markers for the three houses relocated from Linnentown,

(5) Establish a publicly funded Black history center,

(6) Explore policies regulating property acquisitions between the Athens-Clarke County Unified Government and the University System of Georgia,

(7) Establish a state-level authority that could authorize direct payouts for harm done due to all types of discrimination, and that

(8) The county mayor and commission would deliver copies of the resolution to state and federal politicians.

We then identified the decision-makers for the resolution's adoption: Athens-Clarke County Mayor Kelly Girtz and Commissioners Patrick Davenport (District 1), Mariah Parker (District 2), Melissa Link (District 3), Allison Wright (District 4), Tim Denson (District 5), Jesse Houle (District 6), Russell Edwards (District 7), Carol Myers (District 8), Ovita Thornton (District 9), and Mike Hamby (District 10). To convince these individuals to adopt the resolution, we needed to earn the support of our community. To raise awareness, we published our website (redressforlinnentown.com), organized numerous neighborhood meetings, community forums, and several protests at City Hall and UGA, ensured regular press coverage, received letters of support from key organizations and churches, gave personal tours of Linnentown, and encouraged classroom participation of UGA and Clarke County schools.

We gained the support of many important individuals: Georgia State House Representative Spencer Frye (District 118), Attorney Kenneth Dious, Fred Smith, Linda Davis, Rev. Dr. Daryl G. Bloodsaw, Rev. Abraham Mosley. Additionally, several organizations aligned with our movement: Athens for Everyone, Athens Area Democratic Socialists of America, the Athens Chapter of the Libertarian Party of Georgia, the Athens-Clarke County Democratic Committee, East Athens Development Corporation, Historic Athens, United Campus Workers of Georgia (CWA 3265), and the Young Democratic Socialists of America.

The next step was to organize meetings with Mayor Kelly Girtz, Georgia State Representative Spencer Frye, and UGA President Jere Morehead. We needed to tell them the story of Linnentown and the toll the eviction had taken on families, to describe the deceptive partnership formed between the city of Athens and UGA in the 1950s, and to give them data. Joseph knew Representative Frye well, so he set up an appointment. I'd never been outspoken or direct when meeting with politicians before, but I'd made many personnel? adjustments in my past management assignments, so I knew I was capable. I repeated this mantra to push me out of my comfort zone:

"You can do this!"

With the first draft of the Linnentown Resolution in hand, Joseph and I met with Representative Frye in November 2019. At some point during our conversation, we moved from an overview of the neighborhood to my personal story. He listened carefully to make sure he understood everything and showed great compassion as I spoke. Joseph answered Rep. Frye's questions about the data. He listened intently, asked questions throughout, and expressed deep disappointment about what had happened to our community and its residents. He agreed to arrange a meeting with UGA President Morehead and his staff.

True to his word, Representative Frye contacted UGA Vice President of Government Affairs Toby Carr to set up a meeting with University officials, including UGA President Jere Morehead and Linnentown residents. Unfortunately, UGA declined. Undeterred, we directed our efforts to Athens-Clarke County officials.

The second Linnentown Project meeting was held at my house on December 6, 2019. As we had already scheduled meetings with commissioners for the next few weeks, we reviewed the key points we would share with them. Rachelle Berry volunteered to be the Linnentown Project community geographer.

On December 19, Commissioners Mariah Parker and Ovita Thornton met with Rachelle, Joseph, Geneva, and me. We gave a brief overview of the impact urban renewal had had on our community and the activities that had led to its erasure and showed them supporting data. Commissioner Thornton was open to supporting the project once she had received a complete understanding of what had occurred.

In the next meeting, Geneva, Bobby, and I shared our stories with Commissioners Tim Denson and Patrick Davenport. We explained the collaboration between UGA and the city of Athens to expand the UGA campus by demolishing Linnentown, discussed the resolution proposals, and told them the price Athens paid us for our properties: a paltry $216,950.

Next, I met with Commissioner Jerry NeSmith, gave the same impassioned speech, and received his support. Commissioner Parker gave Commissioner Russell Edwards a copy of the resolution, reviewed it with him, and answered questions.

On January 9, 2020, we released the resolution to the public— or rather, we thought we had. Allison McCullick, the director of community relations at UGA who was responsible for publishing the resolution, emailed only the commissioners, instead of releasing the information to the general public. We were infuriated.

Furthermore, her email contained many inaccuracies: for example, it stated that Linnentown had "a racially diverse community." (No, it was 100 percent Black.) Her email also stated, incorrectly, that homeowners "voluntarily" sold their homes, at prices several times higher than the initial valuation. One resident was purportedly awarded $650 dollars for a vacant lot, McCullick wrote, and after appealing, they received $4,420. The lowest amount the city gave was $2,600, she asserted.

Neither claim was true.

Soon after, I met with Commissioner Russell Edwards. UGA was in his district and he had a long-established relationship with the university. He explained that the word "terrorized" in the resolution had put off many of the commissioners and UGA officials. In a follow-up meeting Bobby Crook and I had with him and Commissioner NeSmith, Edwards further commented that the resolution's use of "White supremacy" to describe what had happened decades ago was also not acceptable. Sadly, NeSmith changed his mind—he no longer supported the resolution, but wouldn't say why.

Although we were greatly disappointed, Bobby and I said we were willing to take recommended changes back to the Linnentown Project to review the resolution's wording. We maintained our position that UGA and the city of Athens had intimidated, coerced, and bullied the residents of Linnentown, but we did not use those words.

NeSmith and Edwards agreed to work together on recommending changes to the wording of our resolution to something "softer" and "more acceptable." Bobby and I received an email from them the following week, telling us that legal staff would review their edited resolution and then send it to the commissioners for discussion.

Disheartened and angry, Bobby and I agreed to stop all communications with the two commissioners. In the following weeks,

NeSmith would insist in interviews that he supported the Linnentown Project, had offered to assist us, and even claimed that he "loved" me. However, I no longer trusted him or his motives.

Undeterred, Bobby and I met with Jesse Houle, NeSmith's opponent in the election for commissioner of District 6, my district. He was agreeable, listened carefully to our story, and invited us to reach out to him as needed.

On January 20, we held a peaceful Martin Luther King rally on the steps of the Athens City Hall to plead for justice for Linnentown residents. More than seventy supporters attended and held signs. Commissioners Parker, Denson, and Edwards spoke, although Edwards did not explicitly give his support. The *Athens Banner-Herald* wrote a sympathetic article that included photos of the rally and parade. That helped raise awareness in the city, and we gained further support.

A week later, I held a community forum in District 6. About twenty residents attended, and, surprisingly, so did Commissioner NeSmith. I explained what had happened to Linnentown and told my personal story. I answered questions and reviewed the resolution, especially the seven petitions. NeSmith made some objections; I attempted to politely respond, and then he abruptly left.

The following week, Linnentown descendants attended the mayor and commission's regularly held meeting. A few commissioners were supportive, a few unsupportive, and the rest did not state their position. More than sixty protestors packed the room and we held our signs and banners high. After the mayor and commissioners had concluded discussing items on their agenda, we were allowed to speak for three and a half minutes. Many of us stood in line to speak, and we spoke passionately for more than an hour. When we were done, Commissioners Denson, Parker, Thornton, and Link expressed their support. We needed a total of six votes to pass the resolution.

We continued to hold forums and rallies to garner more support from the Athens community; many attendants volunteered to call their commissioners to ask them to support the Linnentown Project. On February 16, we held our second Linnentown Project meeting, where we selected officers: President Hattie Thomas Whitehead, Vice President Bobby Crook, and Secretary Geneva Johnson Eberhart.

On February 19, David Ragsdale, the department chair of English at Clarke Central High School, invited the first descendants to a forum organized by his students. More than seventy attended, with teachers and administrators standing in the back. The students listened attentively and asked many questions. For most students, this was their first time hearing about urban renewal, and they were astonished that a city had the power to remove a community in the name of "improvement." When some asked how they could help, I told them to call their commissioners and plead for their support.

Audrey Enghauser, lead copy editor for the ODYSSEY Media Group, the high school's news source, did an excellent job interviewing, researching, and covering the Linnentown Project. Their online article "Redress for Linnentown" represented our voices and stories well.

Joseph and I came up with a plan for continuing to raise awareness about Linnentown. We decided to focus on strengthening support by widening our reach to surrounding counties' organizations, directly contacting leaders through emails, in-person meetings, or Zoom. Our focus for the next few months was compiling a list with contact information.

A few weeks after the meeting with Commissioner

Davenport, Joseph received a phone call from him. The commissioner said he had changed his mind and would not be supporting the resolution. A few weeks later, I asked Davenport why he had changed his mind. I was taken aback by his answer.

"I've talked with a few people who thought I should not support it," he said. "I am not supporting and I will do everything in my power to ensure it does not pass."

Nevertheless, I was invited to hold a community meeting in District 1, Davenport's district, on February 23. The commissioner attended. As always, I told my story and answered questions, and some attendees came up to me afterward to ask how they could help. I gave my standard response: "Please call your commissioners and ask them to support the resolution."

I was glad Commissioner Davenport, who stayed until I was done greeting supporters, could see all the enthusiasm we were generating in the community.

While I was lobbying commissioners, I also led tours around the area where our community once thrived. Of course, dormitories stood where Linnentown once did, but I could paint word pictures of my old neighborhood as we walked around the grounds. I described the types of houses that had lined the unpaved streets and how we'd maneuvered the muddy roads after rainy days. I told stories of the residents who had played key roles in supporting other families. I described the flowers that lined the front yard entrances and the enormous magnolia tree on Finley. I believe I could almost get people to smell those fragrant white, pink, and purple blossoms.

I pointed to areas where we had frolicked happily and explained the games we played. I described the play area down by the creek, and that magical swing Abe and his friends had made.

The tours lasted thirty to forty minutes, and they were always the highlight of my day.

On February 24, we spoke at a well-attended meeting in Mayor Girtz's office. Along with the mayor, Commissioners Mariah Parker and Ovita Thornton were there with Joseph Carter, Rachelle Berry, Rev. Abraham Mosley, Rev. Larry Fort, Fred Smith, Krystal Cobran, Geneva Johnson Eberhart, Bobby Crook, and me. We explained that we needed two additional team members with research skills and knowledge of economics to complete our team of five Linnentown descendants and two commissioners. Researchers were needed to calculate the amount of reparations owed to the first descendants. Mayor Girtz and I would coordinate assembling the team in the coming months.

Several days later, Associate Professor of Geography Jerry Shannon invited the Linnentown Project team to his Community Mapping Lab at UGA. Dr. Shannon and his class had been researching and collecting urban-renewal data and constructing a map of Linnentown. We were asked to review their work and to share details of the community and our childhood years there. We sat together at a long oblong table in the middle of the room, while the students sat at tables in a U shape around us and listened to our stories with rapt attention.

What a joy it was to see a map of our erased community! To hold a detailed plot of Linnentown in our hands while describing our community to people who were deeply concerned about the injustices that had occurred—well, that was priceless.

On March 7, we attended the Black History Celebration Michael L. Thurmond Lecture Series, where the Athens Area Black History Committee awarded a Certificate of Achievement to Dr. Joseph Carter and me. The award was called "Significant Contribution to Athens' Rich Historical Legacy: Work with the Linnentown Project." We were greatly honored, but our work was not yet done.

Our indefatigable work continued unabated, and we pressed forward with increased enthusiasm. Commissioner Russell Edwards asked me to speak to the Athens-Clarke County Democratic Committee on March 18, where we had an engaged audience.

Unfortunately, that was the last public meeting we held in 2020, as COVID-19 had begun to spread rapidly throughout Athens and Georgia. Mayor Girtz and the county commissioners passed a stay-at-home ordinance on March 19.

Two months later, the mayor and I felt safe enough to meet outdoors—with masks and six feet between us—to discuss the requirements for a government-funded committee. First, we agreed on a name for our team: the Justice & Memory Project (J&M). Due to the pandemic, we would hold all our meetings via Virtual WebEx. Next, we established the team: Linnentown descendants, a researcher, an economist, and two commissioners.

That fall, on September 2, 2020, the Justice and Memory Project held its first virtual meeting. The attendees included Bobby Crook, chairperson and first descendant; first descendants Christine Davis Johnson, Geneva Johnson Eberhardt, and Freddie Brown Jackson; Charlene Mash, secretary; Professor of Geography Jenn Rice, researcher and parliamentarian; Commissioners Mariah Parker and Mike Hamby; and me, Hattie Thomas Whitehead, chairperson and first descendant. Supporting, non-voting ex officio members were Mayor Kelly Girtz, Manager Blaine Williams, and Krystal Cobran, the first inclusion officer for the Athens-Clarke County Unified Government.

We started the meeting with a moment of silence for Linnentown residents; at every meeting since, we have continued this respectful gesture. We each introduced ourselves and our roles and responsibilities. I organized a subgroup to review the wording of the resolution and bring back a recommendation for approval.

On November 30, 2020, we began our meeting by reading a troubling urban renewal report. Written in June 1968 by UGA social worker Maude W. Keeling, the report was titled "How Far Will $100.00 Go These Days?" Much of the report was disturbing and humiliating. For example, Keeling wrote:

> Such families suffer not only economic poverty but from the depressed view of life it imposes as well. They do not know what a better way of living is, or they have given up any hope of achieving it long ago.

Maude was certainly not describing Linnentown residents, and her condescension was deeply offensive. Our families may have been poor by the world's standards, but we emphatically did not have a "depressed view of life." We had a happy childhood, even idyllic, and the adults of Linnentown were always striving to improve our way of life. We believed in the American dream. We had not given up hope of achieving it—until the government took away our homes and our land.

On December 2, 2020, Commissioner Parker received an email from the county's legal staff with recommended changes to the resolution. County attorneys determined that the third demand in the resolution—direct repayments to Linnentown descendants—would be a violation of the Georgia Constitution Gratuities Clause §VI.6.6., which states, "Except as otherwise provided in the constitution, (1) The general Assembly shall not have the power to grant any donation or gratuity or to forgive any debt or obligation owing to the public, and (2) the General Assembly shall not grant or authorize extra compensation to any public officer, agent, or contractor after the service has been rendered or the contract entered into."

The law was very clear. Either we removed this proposal, reworded it, or changed its entire intent. We had to adopt a different approach that would still provide justice—but what? After a lengthy discussion, we agreed to change the intent of this clause. The new language read:

> The Unified Government of Athens-Clarke County shall, with the approval of the Commission, direct the Linnentown Justice and Memory Committee to determine the total amount of intergenerational wealth lost to urban renewal and, under the Committee's advisement, shall, for as long as the Committee exists under its charge, make annual budgetary recommendations to the Mayor and Commission for operational and capital projects to provide equitable redress, including but not limited to affordable housing, economic development, telecommunication services, public transportation, and public art as redress for past harms caused by urban renewal and to foster future reinvestment in historically underfunded and impoverished neighborhoods in Athens-Clarke County.

This important change would empower Linnentown residents to make annual budgetary recommendations to improve different parts of the city. This would be a form of redress; it would give the Linnentown descendants some sense of justice or atonement for what had occurred to our community.

At our fourth J&M meeting, on January 11, 2021, we unanimously approved the revised resolution and sent it back to the county's legal staff. Dr. Jenn Rice then gave an update on the subgroup's continuing work on the Wall of Recognition. Team member Charlene Mash was asked to research historical markers for the homes removed from Linnentown.

A special meeting of the J&M team was held on January 25, 2021. The county's legal staff had completed the review and recommended formatting of the final version of the resolution. Now, all the team had to do was approve it, and we did, unanimously. The next step was for the resolution to be placed on the earliest Mayor and Commission agenda. Before closing the meeting, I told the team that Mayor Girtz had agreed to write a proclamation for all the erased Black communities in the 1960s recognizing the harmful impact of urban renewal. To have this done in February—Black History Month—was a great way to observe it, and it would be a wonderful way to honor the once-thriving communities of hardworking families and their achievements. This announcement brought tremendous excitement to the entire J&M team!

The Linnentown Project decided to write a letter to the newly elected U.S. Senator Raphael Warnock on January 26, 2021. In this letter, we requested a meeting to discuss assistance on how to address Georgia's gratuity clause and to ask for the opportunity to testify before Congress about our groundbreaking work on reparations.

A few days later, I received a surprising text from Commissioner Mariah Parker that read: "The date for the resolution vote has been moved up to February 16, 2021." It was going to be voted on during a called meeting, just in time for Black History Month! This was great news.

On Tuesday, February 2, 2021, during a mayor and commissioners meeting, Mayor Girtz presented the proclamation. I received a text that evening with a picture of the beautiful document with this heading: "Athens- Clarke County, Apology in Recognition of Athenians Displaced by Urban Renewal Projects." I immediately thought about my mom, dad, and all the other homeowners of Linnentown who I wished could have been there to read this apology.

The proclamation satisfied the first demand in the resolution: a formal acknowledgement of the destruction of Linnentown and other communities through urban renewal. I read through the entire document and greatly appreciated this apology from Athens-Clarke County. I accepted it on behalf of my family and other residents who lived in Linnentown. Healing could now begin, and we could move forward together to build a greater Athens. The following day, descendants and I decided to plan a ceremony that would include the mayor reading the proclamation. This written proclamation was so historic, we thought it would be appropriate to have a ceremony. We planned the ceremony to take place January 22, 2012, at 11:00 a.m. on the steps of City Hall.

Then the moment we had been working toward finally arrived. On February 16, 2021, in a special called meeting of the mayor and commissioners, Mayor Girtz started by thanking everyone for their involvement and support, and gave a summary of our new opportunity to look forward. Commissioner Parker made a motion to adopt the resolution. Those of us from the Linnentown Project were observing via Zoom. We were listening intently as each commissioner gave public input before a voice vote. I started tearing up as I watched, thinking back to the time when my parents and others in the community did not have a voice as they were being pushed out of Linnentown. And then, it happened—the resolution passed unanimously. This was the first official act of reparations in the history of the State of Georgia.

Commissioners Thornton and Russell gave heartfelt comments. Commissioner Russell issued an apology for his failure to support us and believe us. It was unexpected and moving. In previous meetings, he had told me that he did not support the Resolution due to some sharp wording; "White supremacy" and "terrorism" were much too strong, he said. Now he was saying that his judgment had been clouded about what had occurred back in the sixties and that he'd had time to think about it. He also admitted that we and our advocates were telling the truth: it was indeed White supremacy and terrorism carried out by the City of Athens and UGA.

What an amazing change! I thought. *He's made a 180 since our last sit-down discussion.*

Commissioner Thornton expressed gratitude for our work but reminded us there was much more to do—this was just the beginning.

Commissioner Davenport voted for the resolution, but wasn't enthusiastic about it. He cautioned us to not "storm the building" when approaching UGA, to use a softer approach, and throw the university an olive branch. Apparently he didn't know we had written a letter to President Morehead and had had introductory conversations with his staff.

Davenport's next comment stung me. He said the resolution was an "insult" and that Linnentown was being put on a pedestal. He clearly took umbrage with Black people standing up for themselves.

After getting off Zoom and thinking about the resolution passing unanimously, I was filled with happiness and joy. I reached for a copy of the resolution, turned to the page with the list of homeowners and families who had supported and loved me, and stood up. I read their names aloud in my kitchen in the very house that I own. Afterward, I felt as if this action had given voice to them who were voiceless in the 1960s, when their neighborhood was taken away from them. Their voices had finally been heard sixty-plus years later.

But we are far from finished.

Epilogue

When a few young teenagers got an idea to fashion a play area beside a small flowing creek for the younger children, just right outside their community, they had no money, blueprints, equipment, or know-how. What they had was vision, energy, creativity, and a willingness to work hard together as a team to create an almost magical place that has been forever woven into their minds and hearts.

The Linnentown Project set out the same way. There was no previous pathway, no strategy, no money or know-how to seek recognition, redress, and reparations. What we had was a vision to right the wrongs that had been committed more than sixty years ago, the energy to execute a strategy to raise awareness, creativity to draft historic game-changing legislation, and a willingness to stay focused on the work.

I am deeply thankful for and appreciative of Mayor Kelly Girtz for assembling the Justice and Memory Project committee, the first official team in the State of Georgia to work together on avenues of atonement for harms committed against Black communities. The team makeup is historic: first descendants, county commissioners, and citizens, all supported by city staff members.

This type of work cannot be done without what I call "tear-shedding moments." I had two in particular. The first was when the mayor issued our proclamation with an apology—that was astounding. But when he read the proclamation on the top steps of Athens City Hall, I was brought to tears. His words of apology resonated in my spirit. Looking out at the few who attended, including my daughter, I recalled being bussed to jail for demonstrating as a young Black girl back in the '60s. We were on a big yellow school bus that was parked approximately twenty yards from where we were standing at City Hall that day. The tears started flowing—not only for myself but, even more, for all those who were no longer with us. I thought of my parents.

I was moved to tears again while watching the Athens-Clarke County Mayor and Commission meeting on Zoom on February 16, 2020. They were voting to adopt the Linnentown Resolution. With each vote cast, I felt so nervous—until the vote count reached six, the number needed for approval. Before I knew it, the resolution had reached unanimous approval. I was so grateful to be a part of this history-making legislation! After a brief Zoom celebration with family and friends, I said goodbye and closed my computer, picked up the resolution, stood up, and started reading names of homeowners who once lived in Linnentown. I shed tears—happy, joyful tears.

Two other Black communities in Athens were erased due to

urban renewal projects: the Bottoms and Lickskillet. The Linnentown Project and J&M Committee are attempting to locate first descendants who lived in these areas. We're planning to assist as needed with strategies and direct their paths to achieve data. The Linnentown Project is also willing to help other descendants throughout the State of Georgia who lived in thriving communities that were erased due to urban renewal projects. We are committed to help right the wrongs inflicted on low-income Black communities.

I've learned a great deal since being involved and taking a leadership role with both project teams. I've learned how to talk to the press and politicians and how to write legislation and persuasive letters. My direct involvement has deepened my understanding of the need to get state and federal politicians involved in reparations. For example, we need them to take action on the "gratuities clause" in Georgia's Constitution. We've been unable to give direct repayments—including funding affordable housing—due to this clause. We must make these changes to allow for repayments because we must create real, tangible paths to homeownership in order for Black families to be sustainable and build wealth for the future.

I hope to testify before the U.S. Congress about our work. Congress again is talking about HR 40, which establishes a federal commission to study and issue reparations. Black families need to be a part of this. Congressional leaders need to understand the detrimental impact urban renewal had and is still having on low-income families. We were targeted. I want the opportunity to explain how my family and other families' generational wealth was taken from us by law—all in the name of "progress," at the expense of erasing small, low-income Black neighborhoods.

I remember seeing Dr. Martin Luther King, Jr.'s speech on

television in August 1963. His speech was so moving. I watched the large crowds lending support to the movement and each other. I was too young to attend and did not have the money or support to get there, but I made a personal promise to myself: The next time something historic happened at the Mall in Washington, D.C., I would be standing at the reflection pool, giving support. Dr. King was making a difference on a national level—I was attempting to make a difference on a local level. One day, we will fulfill his dream.

Today, when my sisters and brothers and I get together and start talking about things that happened when we were growing up, we always share stories from Linnentown. Although we experienced many challenges and unpleasant treatment, we are thankful for the values and meaning of community that our parents instilled in us. I will continue using these values to work with the Linnentown Project and also with the Athens Step Up Program.

In 2011, after speaking with my siblings, I decided to set up a scholarship program in our mother's name. Mom had completed the eleventh grade in high school before quitting school to work, then married my father, started a family, and kept working. She had a lot of hard jobs during those years and overcame a great deal of obstacles and challenges, including bearing and raising seven children, working a full-time job without complaint, never taking needed time for herself, and getting divorced—all before turning twenty-six. She deserved recognition.

We raised money to establish the Laura Maude Thomas Day Award, a yearly scholarship that would honor her contributions to our family, our community, and our church. In 2012, we were able to award two scholarships to Athens-Clarke County students.

In 2014, my neighbor Joyce Daniels wanted to get involved

and was able to help expand the scholarship. We called the new scholarship the "Athens Step Up Program." Since its inception, we have been able to award over $39,000 to students.

Encouraging, supporting, and advocating for others is what "giving voice" means. It is my hope that you have read this book not only with an educational and social-justice lens, but that you have also been inspired to act. The Linnentown Project has made a call to action to give voice to those who have been wronged, to those whom society has tried to silence, and to those who continue to be affected by systemic oppressions.

Appendix A
LIFE IN LINNENTOWN

Thomas family, circa 1955. Sitting, from left to right: Abe Thomas Sr., Marion, Linda. Standing, from left to right: Katie, Abe Jr., Hattie, Andrew. Not pictured: Laura Thomas and Alexander. *Courtesy of Hattie Thomas Whitehead.*

Row of "shotgun" rental houses with dirt street on South Finley Street, where Hattie was born, circa 1947. Taken from the bottom of South Finley Street looking north toward Baxter Street. Featured in *Joel A. Weir: Film of Athens* (1947). *Courtesy of Walter J. Brown Media Archives and Peabody Awards Collection, University of Georgia Libraries.*

The cheerleading squad at Burney-Harris High School in 1965 (Hattie is kneeling on the far right). *Courtesy of Athens Banner-Herald.*

Hattie at the Burney-Harris High School 1966 senior prom with her oldest brother, Abe, wearing the dress her grandmother made. *Courtesy of Hattie Thomas Whitehead.*

Hattie in her majorette uniform in front of the only telephone pole in Linnentown, 1959. She was in the fifth grade at East Athens Elementary School. *Courtesy of Hattie Thomas Whitehead.*

Rear of Finley Street shotgun rental houses in Linnentown with Baxter Street water tower in background, circa 1947. Featured in *Joel A. Weir: Film of Athens* (1947). *Courtesy of Walter J. Brown Media Archives and Peabody Awards Collection, University of Georgia Libraries.*

Front face of the three-story Jeruel Academy, early 1940s. The Jeruel Academy was later renamed the Union Baptist Institute. It was a prominent Black grammar school that taught Greek, Latin, and the classics, as well as farming and textiles. After integration in 1957, the city of Athens closed the school and destroyed it as part of urban renewal. *Courtesy of Special Collections, University of Virginia Libraries, Charlottesville, Virginia.*

Annual Easter egg hunt at Legion Pool, circa 1954. Left to right: Harriette Ann Powers, Freddie Mae Brown holding Bobbie Powers, Deloris Powers, and Jerome Smith. *Courtesy of Freddie Mae Brown Jackson.*

Brick house on Lyndon Row, circa 1960. Left to right: Bobbie Powers, Harriette Ann Powers, Deloris Powers, and Jerome Smith. *Courtesy of Freddie Mae Brown Jackson.*

Linnentown circa 1943, taken from the old Sanford Stadium looking west toward the Baxter Street water tower. Lyndon Row, where
most of the Linnentown property owners lived, can be seen in the
lower left corner. The intersection of Cloverhurst St. and South
Finley St. is visible in the lower left as well. The Jeruel Academy
appears slightly below the water tower. *Courtesy of Hargrett Rare
Book and Manuscript Library – University of Georgia Special Collections Libraries.*

Fred L. Thomas, Hattie's cousin. Born in Greene County, Fred moved to Linnentown and stayed with his great-grandparents during the summer months. *Courtesy of Freddie Mae Brown Jackson.*

The home of Bobby Crook at 167 Peabody Street, Linnentown, in 1965. This photo was taken from the back of the house, with the newly constructed Brumby Hall dormitory for women in the background. Bobby's house was the last one in Linnentown to be demolished. *Courtesy of Hargrett Rare Book and Manuscript Library – University of Georgia Special Collections Libraries.*

Appendix B
DATA, DOCUMENTS, AND
LINNENTOWN RESOLUTIONS

BLOCK 8
Parcel Number 8

      Date of Acquisition - July 1959
      Purchase Price - Included in Block 8, Parcel Number 1
      Description of Property at time of Acquisition - Known as the Doolittle property, at the intersection of Cloverhurst Avenue and Findley Street, Athens, Georgia, frontage 412' on Findley Street, running back 140', frontage 200' on Cloverhurst Avenue, nine sub-standard buildings.
      Description and Date of any Action taken by the University to Change the Property Since Acquisition - All buildings demolished 1960
      Net Cost or Profit for any Demolition or Removal of Existing Facilities When Purchased - None
      Date and Cost for any Site Improvement Work Since Acquisition (Including Rough Grading, Street, Pavement and Installation of Underground Utilities - None

Date of acquisition and description of the eight "shotgun" houses on S. Finley Street. My family and I lived in one of them before moving to Peabody Street. Mrs. Doolittle was the landlord. (Minutes of Mayor and Council, City of Athens, 3 February 1959, p. 474)

CITY OF ATHENS, GA.

1/5/55 283

by assessed against the abutting property owners in proportion of their lineal foot frontage compared to the entire length of said project.

SECTION 4. All further proceedings in connection with said paving shall be had in the methods provided by the Acts of 1935, and amendments thereto, amending the Charter of the Mayor and Council of the City of Athens.

SECTION 5. All ordinances or parts of ordinances in conflict herewith are hereby repealed.

The following paving ordinance was read and upon motion by Alderman Danner, seconded by Alderman Kimbrell, was declared adopted by unanimous roll call vote:

AN ORDINANCE OF THE MAYOR AND COUNCIL OF THE CITY OF ATHENS, PROVIDING FOR THE PAVING OF   Lyndon Row
CERTAIN PORTIONS OF LYNDON ROW, WATER AND SEWER STUBS, AND FOR OTHER PURPOSES.

BE IT ORDAINED by the Mayor and Council of the City of Athens as follows:

SECTION 1. Lyndon Row in said city shall be paved for a width of twenty feet with double-surface treatment from Cloverhurst Avenue to Church Street with curbing and guttering of concrete for a width of two feet on each side, making twenty-four feet over all.

SECTION 2. Specifications are on file with the City Engineer of the type of material to be used and the method of laying same.

SECTION 3. The actual cost of said paving, curbing and guttering, and water and sewer stubs is hereby assessed against the abutting property owners in proportion of their lineal foot frontage compared to the entire length of said project.

SECTION 4. All further proceedings in connection with said paving shall be had in the methods provided by the Acts of 1935, and amendments thereto, amending the Charter of the Mayor and Council of the City of Athens.

SECTION 5. All ordinances or parts of ordinances in conflict herewith are hereby repealed.

Alderman Danner's request relative to installing street lights on Lyndon Row was referred   Lyndon Row
to the Councilmen from the Third Ward to be handled in their 1955 light appropriation.

Mayor Wells asked the Finance Committee to work out the 1955 street light allotment for   St. light
each ward and report to Council.

The request for a water main on the Whitehall Road was held in committee.

The following ordinance was read and upon motion by Alderman Danner, seconded by Alderman Smith, was declared adopted with Aldermen Danney, Bond, Smith, Kimbrell, Danner, Phillips, Bondurant and Thompson voting yea and Alderman Whitehead and Lovern voting nay:

AN ORDINANCE OF THE MAYOR AND COUNCIL OF THE CITY OF ATHENS, PROVIDING FOR THE RE-PAVING   Oconee St. sidewalk
OF CERTAIN PORTIONS OF THE SIDEWALK ON OCONEE STREET, AND FOR OTHER PURPOSES.

BE IT ORDAINED by the Mayor and Council of the City of Athens as follows:

SECTION 1. The sidewalk on the southwest side of Oconee Street in said city shall be re-paved for a width of five feet with concrete from the Hodgson Oil Refining Company to Williams Street.

SECTION 2. Specifications are on file with the City Engineer of the type of material to be used and the method of laying same.

SECTION 3. The actual cost of said sidewalk re-paving is hereby assessed against the abutting property owners in proportion of their lineal foot frontage compared to the entire length of said project.

SECTION 4. All further proceedings in connection with said paving shall be had in the methods provided by the Acts of 1935, and amendments thereto, amending the Charter of the Mayor and Council of

Ordinance to pave Lyndon Row in Linnentown, approved by Athens City Council, January 1, 1955.

FAMILY SURVEY FORM

CONFIDENTIAL

Block _____ Parcel _____
Structure _____
Dwelling Unit _____ of _____
Site Address _____ Name of Family Head _____

White _____ Owner _____
Non-white _____ Renter _____

Eligible PH _____
Non-eligible _____

Interviewed by _____ Date _____
Checked by _____

A. Structure Survey.
Fill in this section for EACH structure.
 1. Use and type of Construction.
  a. No. of stories _____   b. Condition of structure
                               Dilapidated _____
                               Not Dilapidated _____

  c. Type of Construction   d. Use of structure
     Frame _____   Residential _____
     Brick _____   Commercial _____
     Concrete Block _____   Industrial _____
     Stucco _____   Public _____
     Other _____   Mixed _____

 2. If residence, state number of dwelling units. _____

B. Dwelling Survey.
Fill in this section for Each dwelling unit in this structure.
 1. Is there inside this dwelling;   Yes   No
  a. Cold running water? _____
  b. Hot running water? _____
  c. A flush toilet? _____
  d. If "yes" is c, is it for
     occupants exclusive use? _____
  e. An installed bath or shower? _____
  f. If "yes" is e, is it for
     occupants exclusive use? _____
 2. Is this dwelling adequately heated? _____
    If yes, state type of heating
    equipment _____
 3. Does this unit have adequate lighting? _____
 4. Are all rooms provided with openable
    windows or other adequate means
    of ventilation? _____
 5. Is this dwelling in sound condition? _____
    (Check "no" if dilapidated)
 6. Determination by Enumerator:
  a. Standard if ALL items answered
     "yes" are checked. _____
  b. Substandard if ANY items answered
     "no" is checked. _____

FOR OFFICE USE ONLY   TYPE OF HOUSING NEEDED
1. No. of rooms _____   4. Present rent income ratio _____
   No. of bedrooms _____   5. Ability to pay; (estimate
   All rooms downstairs _____   based on 20% of monthly
   Rooms up or down _____   income (or shelter)
2. Pets? Yes _____ No _____   a. Rent (shelter) per month _____
3. Space needed for cooking purposes?
   Yes _____ No _____ If "yes", explain _____   b. For max payment(incl.
                                                   taxes and in.) per month _____

5-3-66 - Property Acquired thru condemnation -
5-12-66 - House Completely Collapsed - burned
         by Athens Fire Dept.

FAMILY SURVEY FORM   Page 2

C. Family Survey
Family of;   Number in Family _____
  or person has _____   Male under 21 _____
U. S. Citizen _____ Veteran _____ Male under 21 _____
Alien _____   Disabled Vet _____ Total under 21 _____
Serviceman _____   Deceased Vet _____ No. of Roomers, if any _____

Members of family & Other Persons (who will continue to live in household?)	Sex	Age	Source of Income (Wages, Welfare, S.S. Int. Earnings, etc.)	Income per month

Place of employment or person(s)
wage earner _____   Gross Monthly Income $ _____
                               (of family members only)
                               Other Annual Income _____
5a. 1. Classification   outstanding
       Family Eligible PH by Income _____   Secondary Wage Earners
       Approx. PH monthly rent _____   and others allowable
                                             deductions _____
       Non-eligible PH by Income _____   Net Annual Income $ _____

       Indiv. Householders Over 65 _____
       Under 65 _____   PRESENT HOUSING

    Roomer: _____
                               A. Monthly Payments $ _____
 2. Is this family ineligible for   B. Amount of Mortgage
    social reasons (such as   outstanding _____
    law marriage, unmarried mo-   Renter:
    thers, alcoholism, mental   1. Rent per month _____
    ability, exploiting approved   a. Electricity _____
    illegal actions, or delinquency)? b. Gas _____
       Yes _____   c. Water _____
       No _____   d. Heat, oil, etc. _____
    If "yes", explain _____

 3. Dwelling Preferences   I. Gross Monthly Rent $ _____
  1. No. _____ from PH _____
           _____ from FHA _____   3. Rooms occupied by family
           Other _____   or person are:
 2. Wish to apply? Yes _____   Furnished _____
 3. If apparently eligible for   Unfurnished _____
    Public Housing and does not
    wish to apply, why not?   4. No. of rooms _____
    a. Rent too high _____   No. of bedrooms _____
    b. Want privacy _____
    c. Other _____ (explain) _____ 5. Exclusive occupancy by this
                                       family? Yes _____ No _____
 4. Location preferred;   Between _____
    a. Same general part of town _____
    b. Other (list) _____
 5. If private housing preferred,
    approximate (indicate statistics) as
    you propose to pay for standard
    housing $ _____

 5. Based on attitude of person interviewed and other factors does outlook
    for rehousing appear: good _____
                           average _____
                           poor _____

PHRASES: (For each entry in this section, put the number of the item to which
          it applies in the left-hand margin).

Laura Thomas filled out this "Family Service Form" during her interview in 1961. A form was completed by all residents in urban renewal project areas such as Linnentown and gathered families' demographic and economic information. It also included a code enforcement or "dwelling survey" which was used to condemn many houses as "slums," even though most were in good condition. At the bottom of the first page, there is a handwritten office note showing that the Thomas house on Peabody Street was demolished by burning. *Courtesy of Hargrett Rare Book and Manuscript Library – University of Georgia Special Collections Libraries.*

The urban renewal sign at the corner of South Finley Street and Baxter Street, erected by the city of Athens and the University of Georgia. Film of Atlanta Gas Light by Fred Neeley, 1965. Atlanta Gas Light collection, 1957–1989. *Courtesy of Walter J. Brown Media Archives and Peabody Collection – University of Georgia Libraries.*

May 30, 1961

The Honorable Richard B. Russell
The United States Senate
Washington 25, D. C.

Dear Senator Russell:

The City of Athens has filed with the Urban Renewal Adminis-
tration an urban renewal project known as the University Redevelopment Project. This project has been developed by the University and
the City of Athens under the terms of the housing act relative to
college and university urban renewal programs.

This project is extremely important in terms of the growth
and development of the University of Georgia. The area involved is
West of Lumpkin Street and would clear out the total slum area which
now exists off Baxter Street. This project has been approved by the
Regional Office in Atlanta and the University of Georgia has budgeted
the estimated funds necessary for its participation in the program.
I realize that funds will probably not be available until this year's
housing act has been cleared by both houses of Congress and signed
by the President. I would appreciate it, however, if you would assist
us in having this project approved and set up at the Washington level
at the earliest possible time.

With kindest personal regards, I am

Very truly yours,

O. C. Aderhold

A letter to U.S. Sen. Richard B. Russell (R-GA) from University of
Georgia President Omer C. Aderhold that refers to Linnentown (without mentioning its name) as the "total slum area which now exists
off Baxter Street." Russell Hall, which currently exists on the land
formerly occupied by Linnentown, is named in honor of Senator
Russell. *Courtesy of Hargrett Rare Book and Manuscript Library –
University of Georgia Special Collections Libraries.*

Code
R-215   Report on Minority Group Considerations

The University of Georgia Extension Urban Renewal Project will result in a net reduction in the supply of housing available to racial minority families.

1. Extent to which housing in the Project Area is expected to be available to racial minority families.

    The entire Project Area is to be cleared of residential structures and the land reused for public purposes. No housing within this area will be available to racial minority families. As indicated in the Relocation Plan (Code R-223), it is expected that 48 non-white families and individuals will be displaced from the Project Area. These persons now reside in an estimated total of 48 dwelling units. There are 8 vacant non-white residential structures in the area also. Therefore, there will be a reduction of approximately 56 housing units for Negroes due to the University of Georgia Extension Urban Renewal Project.

2. Proposals for provision of housing to replace the reduction.

    There will be 75 new units of public housing for Negroes opened during the proposed relocation period. A development of three bedroom homes has been started in the northeast part of the City and another development of at least twenty homes is expected to start soon. Therefore, there is an ample supply of replacement housing for Negroes.

3. The Athens Citizens Advisory Committee for Urban Renewal was established by the Mayor and Council. The committee which consisted of ten members of which three were colored leaders met with the site occupants for a discussion of the problems concerning the occupants. The Chairman of the Sub-committee for Minority Group and the colored occupants discussed the problem of relocation.

    The Citizens Advisory Committee now consist of 31 members and includes beside the Minority Group Housing Sub-committee a Relocation Sub-committee. In addition to the Negro leadership which has discussed the relocation programming, the past Mayor and the present Mayor have freely discussed the urban renewal project with the minority site occupants. The Negro leadership of the community has indicated that they do not object to the reuse of project land for public purposes and the proposed relocation of Minority families to other areas meets their approval.

The Urban Renewal Program "Report on Minority Group Considerations" was not available to the homeowners of our community. The White establishment handpicked Black men in Athens as leaders and our representatives, even though they didn't live in Linnentown.

Aerial photo of University of Georgia dorms Brumby, Russell, and Creswell Hall (center), circa 1970. The large parking lots behind the dorms sit directly on top of the former Peabody Street and Lyndon Row. The Baxter Street water towers (no longer existing) are visible in the lower left along Baxter. *Courtesy of Hargrett Rare Book and Manuscript Library – University of Georgia Special Collections Libraries.*

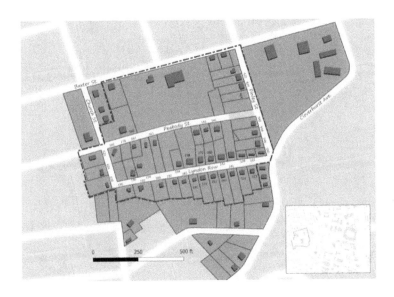

Map created by Dr. Jerry Shannon's Community GIS class at the University of Georgia. Data sources: UGA Special Collections archival records and interviews with former Linnentown residents.

Athens - Clarke County

APOLOGY IN RECOGNITION OF ATHENIANS DISPLACED BY URBAN RENEWAL PROJECTS

WHEREAS, the former City of Athens entered into agreements with the United States Government in the 1960's to create two Urban Renewal Districts, centered respectively on Baxter Street and College Avenue, and

WHEREAS, these two districts featured several hundred residents who were displaced during the decade that followed; and

WHEREAS, despite the intent and expression of "progress" provided at the time, this displacement resulted in the loss of generational wealth, particularly for Black Athenians; and

WHEREAS, social connections, proximity to family, work, leisure education, and entertainment were all lost or diminished by this displacement; and

WHEREAS, Athenians and the Unified Government of Athens-Clarke County are together working toward recognition and remedy for past injustices; and

WHEREAS, this includes the present Linnentown Memory and Justice Committee and will expand to include recognition of other neighborhoods that have been lost; and

WHEREAS, the College Avenue area is again under redevelopment with the explicit intent to utilize a more welcoming and engaging process and an outcome that permanently displaces no current residents.

NOW, THEREFORE, the Unified Government of Athens-Clarke County extends to former residents of Athens' Urban Renewal Districts, their descendants, and to all Athenians a deep and sincere expression of apology and regret for the pain and loss stemming from this time, and a sincere commitment to work toward better outcomes in all we do moving forward.

IN WITNESS WHEREOF, I have hereunto set my hand and caused the seal of Athens-Clarke County to be affixed this 2nd day of February 2021.

Mayor Kelly Girtz
Unified Government of Athens-Clarke County

Formal proclamation apologizing for the harms caused by urban renewal. Issued by Athens-Clarke County Mayor Kelly Girtz, February 2021.

The Linnentown Resolution for Recognition and Redress
Adopted by the Athens-Clarke County Unified Government
February 16, 2021

Resolution in support of recognition and redress for Linnentown, its descendants, and Athens-Clarke County Black communities harmed by urban renewal; acknowledging the City of Athens' collaboration with the University System of Georgia in the destruction of the Linnentown community and the displacement of Black property owners through urban renewal; supporting the establishment of memorials and historical places in honor of Linnentown; supporting the allocation of funds in the annual budget for the economic and community development of historically impoverished communities; calling on the Georgia General Assembly to establish a formal body to address the legacy of slavery and segregation in the State of Georgia and to determine the appropriate forms of material redress:

WHEREAS, as early as 1900, Athens Black families began to settle in a twenty-two acre area called "Linnentown" which was bounded by the currently existing Baxter Street, Church Street, and South Finley Street, and formerly contained the unpaved Lyndon Row and an unpaved portion of Peabody Street on what used to be Judge Newton's plantation land[2];

---

[2] Image 22 of Sanborn Fire Insurance Map from Athens, Clark County, Georgia, Sanborn Map Company, April 1918, U.S. Library of Congress, https://www.loc.gov/resource/g3924am.g3924am_g013771918/?sp=22&r=-0.109,0.297,1.218,0.593,0. *See also* W. W. Thomas, "Map of the City of Athens, GA," 1874, prepared for the Athens Historical Society, University of Georgia Cartographic Services, December 1974, https://athenshistorical.org/product/1874-map-of-athens/.

WHEREAS, from 1900–1960, Linnentown grew to fifty Black families and was a burgeoning and self-sustaining Black neighborhood consisting of skilled members of the Athens community including plumbers, electricians, beauticians, brick masons, housekeepers, and cooks[3];

WHEREAS, Linnentown families were tax-paying residents with decent, albeit low-paying jobs who were building up generational wealth through the ownership of and investment in real property and durable goods;

WHEREAS, in December 1954, Linnentown property owners petitioned the City of Athens to pave Lyndon Row in its entirety and install a street light.[4] By January 1955, the Mayor and City Council approved an ordinance to pave Lyndon Row, and by February 1959, approved additional ordinances to pave Peabody Street, South Finley Street, and Church Street in their entirety, which would have upgraded water and sewage infrastructure and enhanced general accessibility for all Linnentown residents, thereby improving their lives and property values. These

---

[3] See relocation records and family survey forms in *Athens, Georgia, city records, 1860–1970*, MS 1633, boxes 99–100, Hargrett Rare Book and Manuscript Library, University of Georgia Libraries. *See also* folders 10c and 11c for project maps showing 1960 Linnentown property locations. While the city's urban renewal office reported only thirty-seven Black families affected by Project GA R-50, a count of family files and court records shows approximately fifty families. Resident testimony also confirms various occupations: Geneva Johnson Blasingame, personal interview, Athens, Georgia, January 29, 2019; Christine Davis Johnson, personal interview, Atlanta, Georgia, August 31, 2019; Hattie Thomas Whitehead, personal interview, Athens, Georgia, July 31, 2019; and Bobby Crook, personal interview, Athens, Georgia, September 30, 2019.

[4] Minutes of the Mayor and Council of the City of Athens, "Lyndon Row," book 19, p. 271.

ordinances were not followed and the improvements were not implemented for Linnentown residents[5];

WHEREAS, the Housing Act of 1949 established the Federal Urban Renewal Program, which disproportionately affected Black Americans across the United States between 1950-1971;

WHEREAS, in 1959, the Housing Act was amended to allow universities and colleges to participate in the Federal Urban Renewal Program without providing housing for displaced communities;

WHEREAS, between 1959 and 1961, University of Georgia President Omer C. Aderhold corresponded with several local, state, and federal officials, especially Athens Mayor Ralph Snow, University System of Georgia Chancellor Harmon Caldwell, and United States senators Richard B. Russell and Herman Talmadge to request that they leverage political power for the University System of Georgia to obtain a federal urban renewal contract with the

---

[5] Minutes of the Mayor and Council of the City of Athens, *An Ordinance of the Mayor and Council of the City of Athens, Providing for the Paving of Certain Portions of Lyndon Row, Water and Sewer Stubs, and for Other Purposes*, book 19, p. 283. *See also* Minutes of the Mayor and Council of the City of Athens, book 20, pp. 325–326 for additional ordinances providing paving and infrastructural upgrades for Peabody St., Church St., South Finely St., and an amendment to the previous ordinance for Lyndon Row paving. In mid-June 1954, Alderman Kimbrell "requested that Lyndon Row be put on the paving program as soon as possible," ibid., book 20, p. 442. By all appearances, Linnentown was slated to receive equitable infrastructural upgrades with legal and economic support of city council. Nevertheless, personal photographs between 1960–1962 show that Lyndon Row and other Linnentown streets remained unpaved and still without street lights. The ordinances were never implemented and no record of repeals exists. In 1959, the U.S. Housing Act of 1949 was updated to allow universities access to urban renewal funding. Preplanning for Project GA R-50 began as early as August 1961, when the city conducted HUD-mandated preliminary family surveys of the project area.

City of Athens to "clear out the total slum area which now exists off Baxter Street [i.e. Linnentown]"[6];

WHEREAS, the City of Athens and the University System of Georgia have a history within Black communities of acquisition

---

[6] Omer Clyde Aderhold papers, Letter to the Honorable Richard B. Russell from O.C. Aderhold (May 30, 1961), in "Urban Renewal, 1959," UA10–110, University of Georgia Archives, Hargrett Rare Book and Manuscript Library, University of Georgia Libraries, box 59 folder 15. Instead of implementing city ordinances to install infrastructural improvements for Linnentown streets, city officials turned to urban renewal at the behest of UGA officials. On October 14, 1959, Mayor Snow invited federal officials to a city-sponsored luncheon with UGA officialsto discuss "the need for an urban renewal project in an area adjacent to the University campus." Attending this meetingwere "various city officials, President Aderhold, and others with the University." Copied to this letter was Georgia House Representative Julian Cox—Georgia Governor Brian Kemp's maternal grandfather. On November 3, 1959, in a letter to John E. Sims, director of USG's Building Authority, Aderhold confirmed the October 1959 meeting with "federal people, along with our Mayor [Snow], Council, and others." Aderhold and city officials were deciding how to collaborate since UGA could not contract directly with the federal government. No minutes were kept. In early 1961, after a USG Board of Regents meeting in December 1960, Aderhold communicated with USG Chancellor Caldwell about the need to apply for a separate Housing and Home Finance (HHFA) loan of $3.6 million specifically for UGA (in addition to the urban renewal application) in order to fund the construction of the Baxter Street dorms. In this letter, Aderhold named Peabody Street, Lyndon Row, and South Finley Street as slated specifically for the dorms. In consultation with Georgia Assistant Attorney General James Therrell, BOR approved the UGA's urban renewal application with the city of Athens in April 1961. In May 1961 through June 1961, Aderhold communicatedwith Senator Richard B. Russell asking Russell to leverage the application with the federal Urban Renewal Administration. On June 8, 1961, Urban Renewal Commissioner William L. Slayton replied to Sen. Russell to "assure[Russell] that this Agency will approve the application" once funds were available. On June 29, 1961, Senator Herman Talmadge sent a telegram to Aderhold informing of the approval of the $3.6 million federal loan for the "nine-storey [sic] women's dormitory"—Brumby Hall. In August 1961, the City of Athens began preliminary family surveys of Linnentown. The paving ordinances were never repealed and urban renewal had begun. For all Aderhold's urban renewal correspondence, see Omer Clyde Aderhold papers, "Urban Renewal, 1959," in UA10-110, University of Georgia Archives, Hargrett Rare Book and Manuscript Library, University of Georgia Libraries, box 59 folder 15.

of property through eminent domain for the purposes of urban redevelopment, e.g. in 1920, the University of Georgia Board of Trustees minutes allocated

$25,000 to purchase a tract of unspecified Black-owned properties "for the protection of [university] property and the safeguarding of the young women in [the university's] charge,"[7] and then in 1950, a city planning map shows Linnentown as specifically targeted for urban redevelopment[8];

WHEREAS, from 1962–1966, the University System of Georgia contracted with the City of Athens to demolish Linnentown in the name of "slum clearance" in order to erect three "luxury"[9] dormitories—Brumby, Russell, and Creswell Halls—by means of the urban renewal program called the "University of Georgia Urban Renewal Program" or "Project GA R-50." This project operated concurrently with the "College Avenue Redevelopment Project" or "Project GA R-51." Both projects were federally funded through the former Housing and Home Finance Agency (HHFA) which was superseded by the current department of Housing and Urban Development (HUD)[10];

---

[7] Transcripts of the Minutes of the University of Georgia Board of Trustees 1786–1932, volume 7, pp. 179, 199, 210, 226, 263, https://www.libs.uga.edu/hargrett/archives/trustees/trustees%201915-1931.pdf.

[8] J. G. Beacham, City Engineer, *Map of City of Athens*, January 1950.

[9] "Brumby Means Luxury," *The Red and Black*, September 22, 1966, https://gahistoricnewspapers.galileo.usg.edu/lccn/gua1179162/1966-09-22/ed-1/seq-25/#index=0&rows=12&proxtext="Brumby+Means+Luxury%22&sequence=0&words=Brumby+Luxury+Means&page=1.

[10] The Mayor and Council of the City of Athens, Georgia, "University of Georgia Urban Renewal Project GA R-50: Part I — Application for Loan and Grant," Binder No. 3 (May 1962), section R-231 "Legal Data," in *Athens,*

WHEREAS, the City of Athens seized Linnentown properties through eminent domain for as little as $1,450 and families
were displaced to public housing or sporadically throughout the
City of Athens[11];

Georgia, city records, 1860–1970, op. cit., box 35; see also Minutes of the Mayor
and Council of the City of Athens, *Ordinance of the Mayor and Council of the
City of Athens Approving the Urban Renewal Plan and the Feasibility of Relocation
for Project No. GA R-50*, book 21, pp. 463–481; Minutes of the Mayor and
Council of the City of Athens, *Resolution of City Council of Athens, Georgia
Respecting Land Acquisitions Prices for College Avenue Urban Renewal Area,
Project GA. R-51*, book 22, pp. 383–384.

[11] For a vacant lot, Lillie Bell Hunter was awarded only $1,450 by *in rem
condemnation*. She appealed by jury and won $2,500 but still lost the property.
See *Mayor and Council of the City of Athens vs. Vacant lot on the west side of S.
Finley Street, Athens Ga., Lillie Bell Hunter, et al*, Superior Court of Clarke
County, Docket 16384, March 6, 1964. For a lot including a structure, Abbie
Thomas and Callie Jackson (181 Lyndon Row) received the lowest judgment
of $2,600. See *Mayor and Council of the City of Athens vs. 181 Lyndon Row,
Athens, Georgia; Annie B. Thomas and Callie Jackson*, Superior Court of Clarke
County Georgia, Docket 16502, May 14, 1964. However, the overall lowest
judgment awarded was only $650 to Susie Simmons (429 S. Finley) for a vacant
lot on the west side of S. Finley St. She appealed and won $4,420—but still
lost the property. See *Mayor and Council of the City of Athens vs. Vacant lot on
west side of South Finley Street, Athens Ga.; Susie Simmons, Mark Ray and all
other heirs and creditors of Lila Ray deceased*, Superior Court of Clarke County
Georgia, Docket 17660, May 4, 1966; see also docket 16382.

WHEREAS, through intimidation,[12] weaponized code en-forcement,[13] inequitable property value judgments,[14] controlled

---

[12] Before her family relocated, Christine Davis Johnson (193 Lyndon Row) reported active bulldozing in close proximity to her house in the middle of many nights during construction; Christine Davis Johnson, personal interview, Atlanta GA, August 31, 2019. Geneva Johnson Blasingame (123 Lyndon Row) spoke of a meeting her father, Davis Johnson Sr., attended on university campus in late 1962 where he was told his family had "no choice" but to move; Geneva Johnson Blasingame, personal interview, Athens GA, January 29, 2019. Bobby Crook (167 Peabody St.) reported that prior to relocation, piping and other construction material were constantly placed on their property near the house without consent; Bobby Crook, personal interview, Athens, Georgia, September 30, 2019.

[13] See "Family Survey Form — Confidential" in *Athens, Georgia, city records, 1860-1970,* op. cit., boxes 98-100. Even if a property met all code requirements listed, the appraiser had the option to judge if a property were dilapidated. As listed in the family survey, code enforcement question number five asks "Is this dwelling in sound condition?" If *any* item, including number five, were checked "no," then the structure would be condemned as "substandard" or blighted. Using code enforcement, only seven out of approximately fifty Linnentown structures (including rental and non-residential properties) were deemed standard, whereas twenty out of forty white properties in the project area (including rentals) were standard. Compare survey forms for white families, found in box 98, to those of Black-owned properties in *Athens, Georgia, city records, 1860–1970,* op. cit., boxes 98–100. See also Urban Renewal project map dated 3/9/1961 in *Athens, Georgia, city records, 1860–1970,* op. cit., folder 10c. See also "Informational statement," ibid, box 98 folder 1 for criteria for "standard housing."

[14] In Linnentown, thirty-three property owners (out of approximately fifty families) owned thirty-four properties. The average size of a house was five rooms. Not adjusting for inflation, by 1961, the average annual income per Linnentown property owner was $2,150 and the combined annual income for Linnentown property owners was $64,545. The average *in rem condemnation* award was $5,750 with a maximum of $12,250. The overall award value for all Linnentown properties was $195,500. For Linnentown property owners, this implies an *estimated* combined Black wealth (= property award + income) of $260,045. The average wealth for property owners was $7,880. Compare this to white property owners within the GA R-50 project area (Wray St., Hall St., Florida Ave., Waddell St., S. Lumpkin St.). Approximately forty white property owners held forty-five properties (three of which were in Linnentown). The average house size was six rooms. The average annual income for a property owner was $4,900. The combined annual income for white property owners was $93,100. The average *in rem condemnation* award for white-owned property was $13,240 with a maximum of $39,500. The combined award value

demolition by fires,[15] forced tenancy and rent,[16] tokenized Black

---

for all white-owned properties in the project area was $529,500. For white property owners, this implies an *estimated* combined wealth of $622,600 with an average $15,565. Calculating conservatively by percentage difference, then, the average property gap was $7,480 (78 percent) with an average income gap of $2,750 (78 percent), and an approximate wealth gap of $7,685 (66 percent). By 1961, the combined income gap was $28,555 (36 percent) which is comparatively moderate to the other gaps. Nevertheless, individual white property owners in the project area received an average $7,490 (230 percent) *more* for their properties than individual Black property owners in Linnentown. For the raw data, see "Income and Wealth data for Project GA R-50" and "Equity & Gap Analyses," compiled by The Linnentown Project; see also *in rem condemnations*, family survey forms, and relocation records in *Athens, Georgia, city records, 1860–1970*, op. cit., boxes 35; 98–100.

[15] Five properties (141 & 143 Peabody St., 122 & 193 Lyndon Row, and 548 S. Finley St.) were demolished by fire with the assistance of the Athens fire department most likely for training activities. Note that not all residents had been relocated when the fires occurred. Remaining families likely watched their neighbors' houses burn. No white-owned houses in Project GA R-50 were demolished by controlled fires. See *Athens, Georgia, city records, 1860–1970*, op. cit., box 99 folders 22, 23, and 29; box 100 folder 8.

[16] For many Black families in urban renewal, the more dehumanizing aspect of immediate forced tenancy and rent was its stark resemblance to the sharecropping many families had only begun to escape by 1960. Federal urban renewal policies required local public authorities (LPA) such as municipalities to enforce tenancy and charge rent on acquired properties. By 1966, the city collected precisely $28,304.61 in rent payments; see "Citizens Advisory Committee, 1961–66," *ibid*, box 40 folder 5. Any tenant unable or refusing to pay rent was listed as delinquent. Even the Subcommittee on Minority Housing recommended to the program's relocation staff to forcibly evict tenants who refused to resolve delinquent rents; see *ibid*. While both white and Black residents were affected by this policy, the list of delinquent rents were always disproportionately Black. White tenants had the disposable income and were better equipped to relocate far more efficiently and quickly than Black families. This meant less time as a tenant. By August 1966, long after many families had relocated, three white residents—R.E. Gambrell, E.M. Dillard, and L.L. Johnson— amongst eight Black Linnentown residents were listed still delinquent. Gambrell, Dillard, and Johnson owed $169—only 32 percent of the total $529 owed to the city; see "Charge-off of delinquent rent for Project No. GA R-50," *ibid*, box 98 folder 4.

representation,[17] invasions of financial privacy,[18] and paternalistic

[17] Black male property owners willing to participate in and cooperate with the urban renewal project were quickly tokenized by the city and the university in order to show the approval of Athens Black communities like Linnentown. To do this, the city of Athens formed a Subcommittee on Minority Group Housing which reported to the program's Citizens Advisory Committee. The subcommittee members, which varied in size between 1963–1968, consisted of three to five Black male property owners. Project GA R-50 procedures included a 1962 "Report on Minority Group Considerations" that specifies the nature of this subcommittee: "The [Citizens Advisory Committee for Urban Renewal] consisted of ten members of which three were *colored leaders* [who] met with the site occupants [i.e. Linnentown residents] for a discussion of the problems concerning the occupants. The Chairman of the Sub-committee for Minority Group Housing and the colored occupants discussed the problem of relocation. [...] In addition to the *Negro leadership* which has discussed the relocation programing, the past Mayor [i.e. Jack Wells] and present Mayor [i.e. Julius Bishop] have freely discussed the urban renewal project with the minority site occupants. The *Negro leadership* of the community has indicated that they do not object to the reuse of project land for public purposes and the proposed relocation of Minority families to other areas meets their approval" (emphasis added); see "Report on Minority Group Considerations," Binder No. 3 (May 1963), section R-216, in *Athens, Georgia, city records, 1860–1970,* op. cit., box 35. However, handwritten notes and resident testimony show only confusion, disapproval, and distrust amongst Linnentown residents towards the entire project; see *ibid,* boxes 99–100. Again, Geneva Johnson Blasingame reports her father, Davis Johnson, Sr., being told that they had "no choice" but to leave, which left Johnson demoralized and powerless. Ms. Blasingame reports that her father ceased repairing and updating 123 Lyndon Row upon receiving this news. Almost no evidence exists to verify that the city and university held *formal* and *fair* meetings with Linnentown residents. Instead it appears that members of the Subcommittee were tokenized as *ad hoc* "Negro leadership" to serve as a veneer for the approval of Athens Black communities like Linnentown. This was strategic. The city and university would have faced greater risk of violating federal anti-discrimination housing policies had they proceeded with the project if Black residents publicly and legally objected. But since communities like Linnentown already lacked collective political, economic, and legal power, the arbitrary selection of a few Black males by white decision makers intentionally filled a power vacuum for the only purpose of showing the city and university's adherence to civil rights and removing potential roadblocks to the project. The legitimization of Project GA R-50 comes as the cost of Black tokenization. Just one of the intergenerational effects of this type of tokenization is, in turn, the increased accumulation of political power away from Black communities.

[18] Upon learning only recently that the City of Athens and the University of Georgia gathered and kept financial information about residents seemingly without verbal or written consent, Christine Davis Johnson (193 Lyndon Row)

relocation policies,[19] Linnentown was effectively erased without a trace by the City of Athens and the University System of Georgia;

WHEREAS, by 1966, the City of Athens had sold all Linnentown properties to the University System of Georgia for $216,935,[20] and by 2019, the University's current land value plus

---

felt deeply retraumatized by an invasion of financial privacy. Christine Davis Johnson, person interview, Atlanta, Georgia, August 24, 2019. To verify income on Black families, city records show officials checking employer bookkeeping records, social security checks through residents' bank accounts, tax returns, and even checking life insurance policies to verify ages. No written consent or subpoena exists granting approval for these searches. There is no evidence that white families received the same scrutiny. See *Athens, Georgia, city records, 1860–1970*, op. cit., box 99 folders 18–19, box 100 folders 8 and 14.

[19] Urban renewal is paternalism simply by another name. Project GA R-50 is no exception. In fact, as Parkview Extension opened in 1959, the City of Athens and the University of Georgia aimed to relocate many Black families from so-called "slums" to public housing. See The Mayor and Council of the City of Athens, Georgia, "University of Georgia Urban Renewal Project GA R-50: Part I — Application for Loan and Grant," Binder No. 3 (May 1962), section R-223 "Relocation Plan," in *Athens, Georgia, city records, 1860–1970*, op. cit., box 35. Policy was to prioritize public housing for Black families not only as a way to ameliorate poverty and to give communities access to better facilities, but also with the sincere intention to make them more civilized. Tom Hodgson reports that his father, Paul Hodgson, the executive director of the city's Urban Renewal Department, repeated expressed deep frustration at the disapproval and distrust from the Black community toward the project; there was never intentional "malice" and the city wanted to improve the lives of these communities, Hodgson reports (Tom Hodgson, personal interview, Athens, Georgia, August 5, 2019). This, however, assumes paternalistically that Black communities did not and could not understand what was best for them. In fact, this was the official stance of white female social workers hired by the city's Urban Renewal Department to assist the city and the university relocate as many Black populations as possible to public housing. Maude W. Keeling, a social worker for the program, wrote in *The Athens Junior Assembly Reporter* (June 1968) that "By early 1967, about one-half of the relocation caseload consisted of multi-problem families—families who had the least resources of any kind. Such families suffer not only from economic poverty but from the depressed view of life it imposes as well. They do not know what a better way of living is, or they have given up any hope of achieving it long ago"; see "General Correspondence," *ibid*, box 40 folder 16.

[20] Mayor and Council of the City of Athens, *Ordinance of the Mayor and Council*

improvement value of this property totaled $76 million for a return on investment of 35,000 percent with an annualized return of approximately $8.8 million (11.6 percent per annum);[21]

WHEREAS, instead of investing money and resources into Linnentown for it to achieve middle- class status, the City of Athens and the University System of Georgia perpetrated an act of institutionalized White racism and terrorism resulting in intergenerational Black poverty, dissolution of family units, and trauma through the forcible removal and displacement of Black families, and the accumulation of the majority of their wealth and political power within the University System of Georgia and the City of Athens;[22]

---

of the City of Athens Approving the Urban Renewal Plan and the Feasibility of Relocation for Project No. GA R-50, book 21, pp. 478. To resolve the $1.1 million federal loan to the City, the Board of Regents of the University System of Georgia (BOR) paid only the "average appraisal figure" of $216,935 as final sale value ("land disposition appraisal") to the homeowners? for all Project GA R-50 properties. This value was calculated after the application of forty-six noncash grant-in-aid credits ("Section 112 Credit") or land swaps with BOR which totaled $864,885. This was permitted by the 1959 amendment to the 1949 Housing Act (73 Stat. 677, 42 U.S.C §1463 Suppl. 1959). For an explanation of these credits, see also Ashley A. Foard & Hilbert Fefferman, "Federal Urban Renewal Legislation," *Law and Contemporary Problems*, 25 (4), pp. 680–681.The University began purchasing these properties in June 1955, likely in preparation for the project. This allowed BOR to purchase Linnentown property using as little cash as possible and in turn enabled the city to accumulate more land—most of which were formerly Black-owned. See Mayor and Council of the City of Athens, *Ordinance*, book 21, pp. 468–472.

[21] According to the Athens-Clarke County Tax Assessor, the University System of Georgia Board of Regents owns the area currently occupied by Brumby and Russell Halls (parcel 170 001N), which was formerly Linnentown. As of 2019, the land value alone is $4.33 million. Including improvements (i.e. dorms, parking lots), it is $75.95 million. See "Summary: Parcel Number 170 001N," https://qpublic.schneidercorp.com/Application.aspx?AppID=630&LayerID=11199&PageTypeID=4&PageID=4601&KeyValue=171%20%20%20%20001N#.

[22] Hattie Thomas Whitehead reports that her mother and father divorced immediately following displacement. For the effects of intergenerational trauma and mental health problems in Black communities resulting from urban

WHEREAS, a total of 176 Black families compared to 122 White families were displaced by both Project GA R-50 and R-51 between 1962–1974, which shows that a disproportionate number of the Athens Black population were affected by urban renewal in Athens, Georgia and that urban renewal strategically targeted Black communities like Linnentown through dispossession and erasure;

WHEREAS, between 1959 and 1974, over 70 universities and colleges in the United States received federal funding for urban renewal, including the University of Georgia, Georgia State University, Georgia Tech University, and the Medical College of Georgia, which displaced 324 Black Americans in the State of Georgia from 1961–1974;[23]

WHEREAS, in the words of the activist James Baldwin said, "Urban renewal is negro removal,"[24] the erasure of Linnentown is a key example of larger patterns of collaboration between public institutions of higher education and federal, state, and local government agencies to seize and dispossess Black-owned properties,

---

renewal, see Mindy Thompson Fullilove, "Root Shock: The Consequences of African American Dispossession," *Journal of Urban Health* 78 (1), pp. 72–80. See also Mindy T. Fullilove and Rodrick Wallace, *Collective Consciousness and its Discontents: Institutional Distributed Cognition, Racial Policy, and Public Health in the United States* (Springer, 2008). For the effects of economic and political destabilization through urban renewal as told through oral histories, see James Robert Saunders and Renae Nadine Shackelford, *Urban Renewal and the End of Black Culture in Charlottesville, Virginia* (MacFarland, 1998).

[23] Raw data provided by Robert Nelson, Director of the Digital Scholarship Lab and Head of Digital Engagement in Boatwright Library at the University of Richmond.

[24] James Baldwin, Interview on WNDT-TV, New York City, May 28, 1963.

which reflects the legacy of slavery and Jim Crow in both Athens, Georgia, and in the United States at large;[25]

WHEREAS, on September 14, 2019, Athens-Clarke County Mayor Kelly Girtz publicly stated that properties in Linnentown "would be worth hundreds of thousands of dollars each if preserved in their original locations, and an asset those families would have been able to rely upon to build wealth";[26]

WHEREAS, in 2019, Congress passed H.R. 40 "Commission to Study and Develop Reparation Proposals for African-Americans Act" which establishes a commission to examine the socio-economic effects of slavery and to recommend appropriate remedies;

WHEREAS, between 1989 and 2020, at least seven municipalities (Asheville, NC; Chicago, IL; Detroit, MI; District of Columbia; New York, NY; Philadelphia, PA; and San Francisco, CA) and seven state legislatures (California, Maryland, Michigan, New Jersey, New York, and Texas) have adopted resolutions acknowledging the legacy of slavery and calling for reparational remedies for the lasting effects of segregation and racial violence;[27] and

---

[25] For general trends in the racialized effects of urban renewal across the United States, see the interactive mapping project *Renewing Inequality* (https://dsl.richmond.edu/panorama/renewal/). See also N. D. B. Connolly, *A World More Concrete: Real Estate and the Remaking of Jim Crow South Florida* (Chicago: University of Chicago Press, 2014). For the connection between urban renewal, *de jure* segregation, and redlining, see Richard Rothstein, *The Color of Law: A Forgotten History of How Our Government Segregated America* (Liveright, 2017).

[26] Athens-Clarke County Mayor Kelly Girtz's Facebook page, accessed September 14, 2019, https://www.facebook.com/MayorGirtz/.

[27] Michael T. Martin and Marilyn Yaquinto, eds., *Redress for Historical Injustices in the United States: On Reparations for Slavery, Jim Crow, and Their Legacies*

WHEREAS, this resolution results from research funded by the Athens-Clarke County Mayor's Office through an internship provided by its Community Improvement Program grant and fully supported by The Linnentown Project, a community-led project headed by former Linnentown property owners to celebrate the history of Linnentown and to educate the Athens community about the legacy and impact of urban renewal in Black communities;

NOW, THEREFORE, let it be resolved by the Mayor and the Commission of Athens-Clarke County, Georgia, that:

Section 1. The Unified Government of Athens-Clarke County acknowledges the fundamental injustice and resulting harm to Linnentown and other Black communities as a result of urban renewal by the City of Athens and the University System of Georgia.[28]

Section 2. The Unified Government of Athens-Clarke County,

(Duke University Press, 2007), pp. 219–259; see also Resolution No. 20, "Resolution Supporting Community Reparations for Black Asheville," Asheville City Council, July 14, 2020.

[28] The demand for reparations extends well beyond the descendants of slavery precisely because the effects of slavery do not end in 1865. White terrorism and Black oppression are recodified and rematerialized throughout the 20th century through lynching, Jim Crow, redlining, and urban renewal. The lasting effects can be seen today with intergenerational poverty, *de facto* housing segregation, displacement/gentrification, and nearly irreconcilable wealth gaps. See William Darity Jr and Dania Frank, "The Political Economy of Ending Racism and the World Conference against Racism: The Economics of Reparations," in *Redress for Historical Injustices in the United States: On Reparations for Slavery, Jim Crow, and Their Legacies* (Duke University Press, 2007), pp. 249–254 and Roy L. Brooks, *Atonement and Forgiveness: A New Model for Black Reparations* (University of California Press, 2004).

in partnership with Linnentown residents, shall seek to establish a partnership with the University System of Georgia to recognize the history and legacy of Linnentown and its descendants through the installation of an on-site "Wall of Recognition."

Section 3. The Unified Government of Athens-Clarke County shall, with the approval of the Commission, direct the Linnentown Justice and Memory Committee to determine the total amount of intergenerational wealth lost to urban renewal and, under the Committee's advisement, shall, for as long as the Committee exists under its charge, make annual budgetary recommendations to the Mayor and Commission for operational and capital projects to provide equitable redress, including but not limited to affordable housing, economic development, telecommunication services, public transportation, and public art as redress for past harms caused by urban renewal and to foster future reinvestment in historically underfunded and impoverished neighborhoods in Athens-Clarke County.

Section 4. The Unified Government of Athens-Clarke County shall designate as historic any and all relocated Linnentown structures, erect applicable historical markers, and apply to register them with the National Register of Historic Places.

Section 5. The Unified Government of Athens-Clarke County shall seek partnership with the University System of Georgia to create and co-fund a local Center on Slavery, Jim Crow, and the Future of Athens Black Communities.

Section 6. The Unified Government of Athens-Clarke

County shall explore policies regulating property acquisitions by and land swaps between the Unified Government of Athens-Clarke County and the University System of Georgia, including but not limited to policies requiring additional fees in lieu of taxes for any property acquisition by public entities.

Section 7. The Mayor and Commission of Athens-Clarke County urges the Georgia General Assembly to establish an Authority on Recognition & Redress for the purpose of formally acknowledging Black communities harmed by slavery, Jim Crow segregation, redlining, and urban renewal in the State of Georgia; and to determine the appropriate forms of compensation to redress the loss of intergenerational wealth and property as the result of historically discriminatory policies and practices.

Section 8. The Mayor and Commission of Athens-Clarke County requests that the Office of Intergovernmental Relations deliver copies of this resolution, upon adoption, to Governor Brian Kemp, Georgia State Senators Bill Cowsert and Frank Ginn, Georgia House of Representatives Spencer Frye, Houston Gaines, and Marcus Wiedower, United States Representative Jody Hice, United States Senators Raphael Warnock and Jon Ossoff, the University System of Georgia Executive Director of Government Relations Casey Tanner, and the University of Georgia Vice President of Government Relations Toby Carr.

SO RESOLVED, this ____day of _____, 2021.

APPROVED:

Kelly Girtz, Mayor

ATTEST:

Jean Spratlin, Clerk of Commissions

Appendix C
INTERVIEWS WITH THE LINNENTOWN PROJECT

Dr. Carter, PhD, is the project leader of the Linnentown Project Team who was instrumental in getting the data on the erasure of Linnentown as part of the Urban Renewal Project No. GA R-50.

The interview with Dr. Joseph ("Joey") Carter allowed him to share personal information about himself that isn't captured in this book. It helps explain why he was asking questions about how UGA had vastly expanded in previous years, and at what expense to landowners in the city. Dr. Carter shares his personal feelings upon learning of a Black community that was demolished, how he arrived at his decision to start researching this growth, and about his willingness to continue researching when realization of the scope of work had broadened to the point that assistance was needed. He explains how he located the data that had been archived for so many years, how he reached out to the community for assistance in locating first descendants, and how he prepared himself to meet each one individually. He talks about the personal impact of listening to and learning about the families as they shared personal stories and pictures, and of the bond he formed with these families. He also explains his involvement in organizing and drafting the resolution and speaks of his goals, accomplishments, and future plans.

Rachelle Berry worked with the Linnentown Project as the project's community geographer. She helped with organizing the first descendants and explained to them the work it would take to get the resolution passed.

In her interview, Ms. Berry explains how she met Dr. Carter and how she assisted him in locating and researching documents. She shares how she felt upon learning about the erasure of the Black community off Baxter, her involvement with the project, and the contributions she made in drafting the resolution. She describes the initial meeting with the first descendants, listening and learning while they shared their personal stories, and her hopes for the resolution in the future.

INTERVIEW WITH DR. JOSEPH CARTER

Hattie: What brought you to Athens?

Joey: I came to Athens in 2006. I transferred to the University of Georgia to finish my undergraduate degree in philosophy and classics. In 2018, I earned my PhD in Philosophy of Science from UGA. I am also a certified labor researcher from the School of Industrial and Labor Relations at Cornell University.

Hattie: How did you learn about a small African American community off Baxter street that was erased in the sixties?

Joey: At the beginning of my research in the fall of 2018, Athens-Clarke County Commissioner Melissa Link (District 3) mentioned to me she heard "rumblings" of a Black neighborhood off of Baxter St. where Brumby, Russell, and Creswell dorms are currently located.

Hattie: What was the driving force behind you researching its erasure?

Joey: Originally, my research more broadly concentrated on determining how the University of Georgia plays a substantial role in systemic low wages, rising property values, and accelerating gentrification in Athens. My work was connected to labor research I was conducting for the United Campus Workers of Georgia (CWA 3265). After learning about Linnentown, however, I refocused my work on the history and effects (legal, economic, familial, and traumatic) of urban renewal on Black communities and its connection to institutions of higher education.

Hattie: How long into the research did you get an indication as to what had occurred?

Joey: In late 2018, as soon as I discovered archival material on urban renewal at the UGA Special Collections library, I had a sense immediately that the university had something to do with this community's (whose name was unknown to me at first) displacement and erasure.

Hattie: How did this make you feel, and why did you decide to continue?

Joey: Angry, coming off the heels of Baldwin Hall organizing. There was a lot of anger about how the University gaslit organizers and the community. I was also afraid of speaking too early and losing the archives which pushed me to do the research independently and keep it quiet until I met with the residents. It was only after the historic Athens brown bag that I was sure it was time to make the project open and public.

Hattie: When did you decide it was time to reach out to the community to try and locate descendants that had lived there and how did you go about this?

Joey: It was early January 2019 I sat down with Melissa Link to share the archives I had found. I came with the names of all the families and that's when Melissa said she knew someone who could put me in touch with Geneva Blassingame. When I met Ms. Blassingame, I brought her file from the archives and it was her first time seeing it and I knew the magnitude of the research and the project. None of these residents had seen the files or the court hearings and didn't know about these records of their lives that were sitting in the vault on their family. It was through Geneva that I met the rest of the residents and I gave each one of them a copy of their file.

<u>Hattie</u>: How long did it take for you to meet a descendent? Moving from paper to a person, how did you feel during and after this meeting?

<u>Joey</u>: I started the research on paper in early fall 2018 and then met Geneva January 2019. It took about four to five months. I had no expectation of finding anyone and looking at the displacement patterns I didn't know. I was overwhelmed by meeting Geneva and sat in the car dumbfounded after hearing that she's still living in a house from Linnentown.

<u>Hattie</u>: When and how did you learn the name of the community?

<u>Joey</u>: My first meeting with Geneva I told her what I had been calling the community—"Jeruel community"—based on the local Black school. I asked her the actual name of the community and I repeated the name back to her. And she said, "You say it like a White man." And she elaborated on the importance of the spelling and pronunciation. The name distinguished it from the name of the street which was named after a White man. She even spelled it for me which was different from the street: Lyndon Row.

<u>Hattie</u>: After meeting other residents, how did you feel about the

work you had done?

Joey: Overwhelmed and excited. I had no idea I would meet even one of the residents and instead I met an entire community.

Hattie: What did you learn from the residents that had occurred that was most enlightening and disappointing?

Joey: The story that Geneva tells of her father going to a meeting at UGA and his nickname was "Snowball," not an endearing nickname. He was told he did not have any choice but to leave. This story showed me how little self-determination Black families had.

Hattie: After the residents started meeting and wanted to move forward for Justice, what role did you play drafting the Resolutions?

Joey: I played the primary role in drafting the document into policy language and inserting all of the footnotes as supporting evidence. Six pages worth of footnotes that overwhelm the reader with evidence of this tragedy.

Hattie: How long did it take you to complete the research on Linnentown?

Joey: It took about a year to complete the research necessary for the resolution, but there is still more to be done.

Hattie: Did you reach out to anyone for assistance?

Joey: Steven Brown (former UGA Archivist), Kelly Girtz for grant money, Robert K. Nelson (Project Director for Renewing Inequality, University of Virginia), Tommy Valentine (Historic Athens), Fred Smith (East Athens Development Corporation)

Hattie: How did you become project leader?

Joey: I became the project leader by virtue of leading the research and the organization.

Hattie: How do you feel with what has been accomplished thus far?

Joey: Grateful for the opportunity to work closely with all of the residents and to learn from them and to see them come together to write their own story about what happened to them. But also, still very cautious about the city's engagement and knowing how city officials will try to water down any demands that are made of them so we still need to be persistent in fighting for what the residents want and deserve.

Hattie: As project leader, what are your hopes for the resolutions in the future?

Joey: My hope is that the resolution passes as written and that the demands within the resolution are met to the residents' satisfaction, and that this is a model for other communities inside and outside of Athens.

INTERVIEW WITH RACHELLE BERRY

<u>Hattie</u>: What brought you to Athens?

<u>Rachelle</u>: UGA brought me to Athens. I was disillusioned with the world after Trump, so I decided to get a PhD in Geography at UGA and hide out for a few years in Athens until I decided what to do.

<u>Hattie</u>: How did you learn about a small African American community off Baxter street that was erased in the Sixties?

<u>Rachelle</u>: Joey Carter discovered this data and needed a geographer for the Linnentown Project.

<u>Hattie</u>: What was the driving force behind your researching its erasure?

<u>Rachelle</u>: After Baldwin Hall organizing, Linnentown seemed just as important to bring light to the city and to show that UGA was just as to blame for Linnentown's erasure as its history of slavery.

<u>Hattie</u>: How long into the research did you get an indication as to what had occurred?

<u>Rachelle</u>: I was already well versed in Urban Renewal. I studied UR in Detroit and Syracuse; it's been a core part of my academic work. So as soon as we had the first meeting and heard the residents speak about what happened to them, I could easily determine what happened. What was unique was to discover how the

university and the city worked together to erase the neighborhood.

Hattie: How did this make you feel, and why did you decide to continue?

Rachelle: I was angry. They deprived Athens of having an upper-middle class neighborhood. I was very familiar with the politics of UGA and they work through shame. So, the only way to get them to admit that they did something wrong was to be as vocal as possible about it.

Hattie: When did you decide it was time to reach out to the community to try and locate descendants that had lived there and how did you go about this?

Rachelle: This was more of Joey's role. I played more of a role in work within and against the university in trying to get reparations, such as how to frame our demands in the resolution.

Hattie: How long did it take for you to meet a descendent? Moving from paper to a person, how did you feel during and after this meeting?

Rachelle: I met Freddie Mae at the Lyndon House discussion in 2019. I was sitting beside her and struck up a conversation with her. It was eye opening to understand the loss, and just how big of a loss—not just personally—for the whole Black community. It wasn't until this that I didn't quite understand the magnitude for the whole community until meeting residents of Linnentown. What was evident about Linnentown was that it was an up and coming neighborhood, and that potential was lost. It was a blow to the whole Black community to lose such an opportunity for an anchor. If you think of someone like Geneva Blassingame, it was yet another time where they had to start over, another episode of land loss for Black persons in Athens. Black persons coming from the rural areas outside Athens after slavery were already losing land. So, when coming to the more urban areas, settling, and only to lose land again—it was a huge blow to generations of Black families.

<u>Hattie</u>: When and how did you learn the name of the community?

<u>Rachelle</u>: From Geneva Eberhart.

<u>Hattie</u>: What did you learn from the residents that had occurred that was most enlightening and disappointing?

<u>Rachelle</u>: For me it was how they were professionals; they built their own homes, neighborhood integration with generations of families, which is something Black communities don't really have today. To lose a neighborhood that had so much wealth of resources—wealth of people who were highly connected and skilled.

<u>Hattie</u>: After the residents started meeting and wanted to move forward for Justice, what role did you play drafting the Resolutions?

<u>Rachelle</u>: Support the group discussions that brought the stories out to put into the resolution; using my understand about Black political thought, I helped Joey take the stories that were shared and put into language that respects the Black experience and speaks about UR and White supremacy in policy.

Hattie: How long did it take you to complete the research on Linnentown?

Rachelle: It's not really complete. Joey did so much grunt work and then students did a lot of the initial work the students did geography and mapping.

Hattie: Did you reach out to anyone for assistance?

Rachelle: My connection to Community Mapping Lab run by Jerry who is on my committee and people knowing that I do Black geography with my background with Black political thought and organizing.

Hattie: How do you feel with what has been accomplished thus far?

Rachelle: I feel excited and nervous for the committee to go in and put together what needs to be done for reparations. Excited for work that's been done: getting the community on board to support Linnentown, getting Linnentown residents to organize for their needs, that they told the city what happened to them--that in of itself is a win. We need more of these generational organizing efforts. Fearful of the Mayor and Commission to obfuscate efforts to win the resolutions.

Hattie: As community geographer, what are you hopes for the resolutions in the future?

Rachelle: My hope is that residents get everything they want as fast as possible. I hope they publish the resolution as close as possible to the exact experience of the residents. I hope that the fears of White men on the committee do not override the voices of residents.

References

Athens, Georgia, city records, 18601970. MS 1633. Boxes 99–100. Hargrett Rare Book and Manuscript Library – University of Georgia Libraries.

"Brumby Means Luxury." *The Red and Black*. September 22, 1966. Retrieved from Georgia Historic Newspapers, October 14, 2019.

The Mayor and Council of the City of Athens, Georgia, "University of Georgia Urban Renewal Project GA R-50: Part I – Application for Loan and Grant," Binder No. 3, May 1962.

Minutes of the Mayor and Council of the City of Athens. Accessed 2019.

"Redress for Linnentown." www.redressforlinnentown.com. 2021.

For more information on the Athens Step Up Program, please visit www.athensstepup.com.